COMMUNICATION

BY

OBJECTIVE

HOW NON-PROFIT ORGANIZATIONS CAN BUILD BETTER INTERNAL AND PUBLIC RELATIONS

L. ROBERT OAKS, APR

GROUPWORK TODAY, INC.

Post Office Box 258
South Plainfield, N. J. 07080

Published by **GROUPWORK TODAY, INC.**
P.O. Box 258
South Plainfield, N. J. 07080
ISBN NO. 0-916068-03-X

Library of Congress catalog number 76-27996

Copyright (c) 1977 by L. Robert Oaks. All rights reserved No part of this publication may be reproduced in whole or in part in any means, electronic, mechanical photocopying or otherwise without permission by the publisher. Short quotes by reviewers are allowed without permission.

Printed and bound in the U.S.A.

ACKNOWLEDGEMENTS

Gratitude is hereby expressed to the many friends and acquaintances whose shared experiences and inspiration have made this book possible. In particular I wish to thank Harry E. Moore, Jr., at whose suggestion the book was written; Dr. William G. Johnston, of Iona College; Frederick I. Daniels, retired social agency executive; Dr. James E. Barron, management education specialist; Merrill Cochran Phillips, APR, and Thomas M. Wolff, APR, public relations counselors; Marshall Sewell, Jr., APR, Muhlenberg Hospital; the Rev. Dr. Homer L. Trickett, First-Park Baptist Church; and representing the social agencies: Theodore Blum, Somerset County 4-H Clubs; Mrs. Betty Cohen, Washington Rock Council, Girl Scouts of America; Barry Hantman, Plainfield Jewish Community Center; Furman B. Phelps, King's Daughters Day Nursery; Joseph Qutub, Scotch Plains-Fanwood Y.M.C.A.; William Scollay, Watchung Council, B.S.A.; Mrs. George Shuman, Plainfield Senior Citizens Center; Mrs. Angie Shunaman, Plainfield Y.W.C.A.; Mrs. D. Kenneth Sias, American Red Cross; and Richard Snead, Plainfield Area Y.M.C.A. Especially I wish to thank my wife, Mathilda R. Vaschak, M.D., whose forbearance has enabled me to write this.

L. ROBERT OAKS

COMMUNICATION BY OBJECTIVES PLANNING CHART

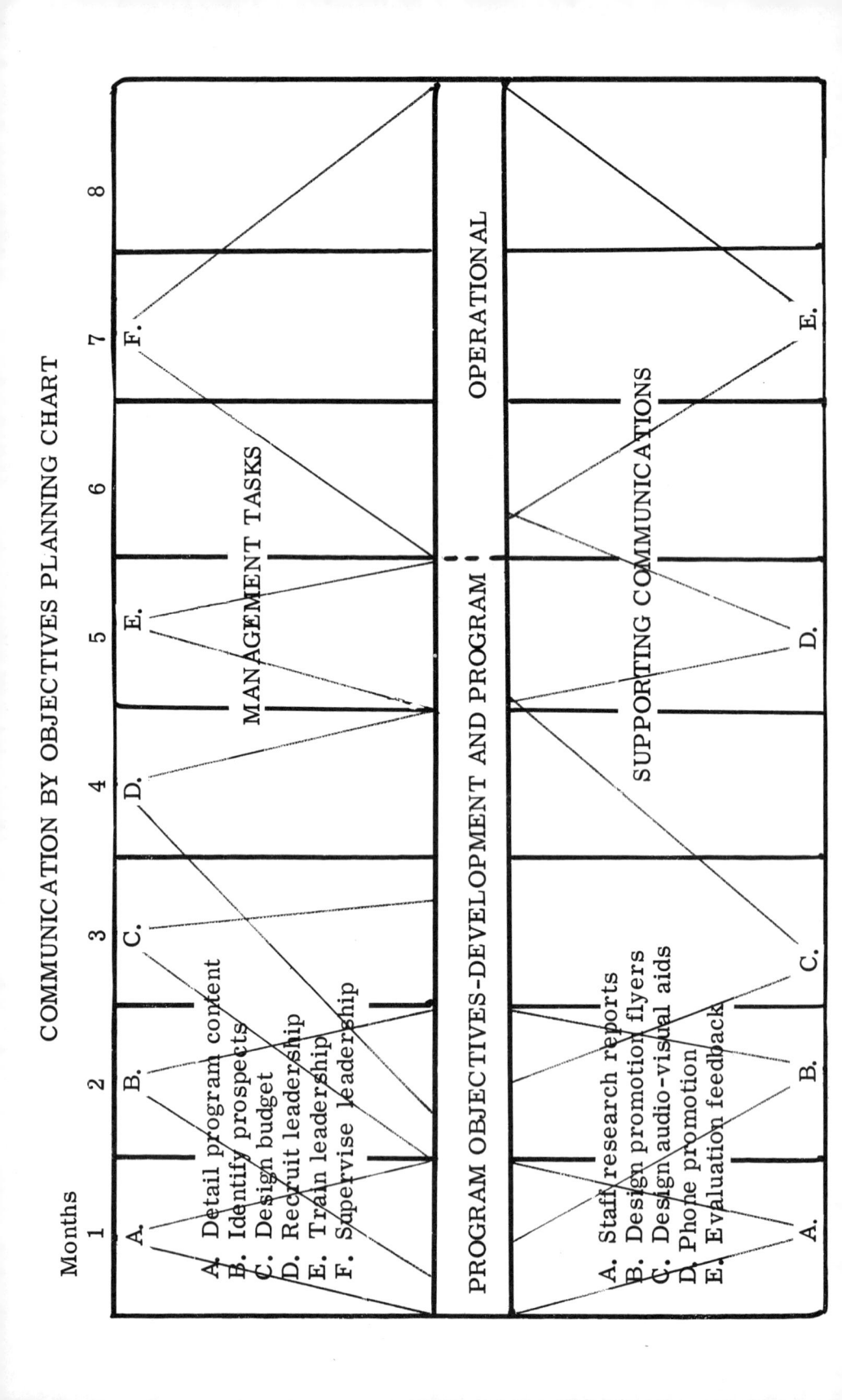

Months: 1 2 3 4 5 6 7 8

PROGRAM OBJECTIVES – DEVELOPMENT AND PROGRAM / OPERATIONAL

MANAGEMENT TASKS

A. Detail program content
B. Identify prospects
C. Design budget
D. Recruit leadership
E. Train leadership
F. Supervise leadership

SUPPORTING COMMUNICATIONS

A. Staff research reports
B. Design promotion flyers
C. Design audio-visual aids
D. Phone promotion
E. Evaluation feedback

INTRODUCTION

"My purpose in this next hour will be to show you how to increase your salaries."

With this opening, a top communication executive of one of the world's largest corporations captured the full attention of his audience. The occasion was a symposium on management communication, held in New York's Waldorf Astoria Hotel, with middle management of large and small companies across the United States as participants.

The meeting, which occurred many years ago, was a groundbreaking effort, and the opening address achieved something of a reputation as a classic. The speaker held his audience's attention from the beginning as he explained how more effective communication could make their work more valuable to their employers. He stressed communication in three directions: to those they supervised, to fellow managers on whose cooperation their own success would depend, and to the executives to whom they were responsible.

The speech was in itself an example of good communication—well-organized, replete with examples of everyday communication problems and opportunities, and limited in length to leave time for questions from his audience. The speaker stressed what have since been accepted as communication axioms—clear, specific statements in terms the listener understands and accepts, relating the individual's and the organization's goals to a common purpose, listening and considering the other's response. He showed how such communication could improve productivity, morale and the organization's reputation for integrity and fair dealing.

This was years before social scientists discovered the employee's need for self-fulfillment and public relations specialists conceived the corporate image. However, in retrospect, the address seems to have hinted at a number of such modern developments. Certainly it excited those who heard it with glimpses of what the future of the public relations function might become.

Since then, "communication" has become an innovative and fast-growing profession, with increased professionalism, status, and recognition from top management. Its nature has been altered by advancing technology and changes in media. It has spawned numerous specialties. But, functionally, a principal division has grown between external communication, or public relations, and internal communication, or employee relations. Regardless of such fragmentation, there is a need for overall planning and coordination of communication at the highest organizational level.

Without central direction of its communication, an organization may acquire, and deserve a reputation for hypocrisy. One such organization which, in its communications to the public, made a brilliant advocacy of enlightened employment practices faced a revolt from its own staff. Its chief executive neglected internal communication and ignored his employees' complaints. This resulted in a loss of credibility with the publics to whom he looked for support and to failure to gain acceptance of his program.

A development of the past several decades is **management by objectives**. Also, there has been a striving by communication professionals to fix goals, plan use of personnel and other resources, set time schedules in support of management objectives and deadlines, provide yardsticks by which communication achievement can be assessed, and build feedback into the communication process. The result is to reduce the vagueness and eliminate the mystery formerly associated with much of public relations. It makes it a more effective support for management.

The purpose of this book is to provide guidelines for executives and professionals in the present-day communication environment, together with examples of innovative and efficient communication in support of institutional objectives.

L. R. O.

TABLE OF CONTENTS

Chapter	Title	Page
I	Communication—Essential Management Ingredient	1
	Communication by Objective	2
	Management and Communication	4
II	Image-Building—A Long-Range Objective	5
	Establishing an Ideal Image	5
	Guidelines Use With Fuzzy Image	7
	The Value of a Symbol	8
	How Does Your Image Rate?	9
III	Communication—Lifeblood of an Organization	11
	Communication Begins at the Center	12
	Snafu at the Youth Center	12
	Enlarging the Information Circle	13
	Continuing Communication with Board Is Vital	14
	Orientation for the New Trustee	15
	Planning Is Essential to Communication Success	16
	Communication That Was Handicapped	17
	Planning to Reach an Objective	18
IV	External Communication—Generator of Community Support	22
	Four Objectives of Communication	22
	Improving the Communication Climate	23
	Building an Image Is Endless Task	24
	Case of Lost Identity	25
	Foundation's Face-Lifting	26
	Steps for Building Institutional Image	28
	Keeping the Image Current	29
	Communicating New Problems	30
	Keep the Information Flowing	32

Chapter	Title	Page
V	Delegating Communication Responsibilities	33
	Picking a Public Relations Person	34
	Orientation of the New PR Person	35
	Planning PR Program and Setting Priorities	36
	The PR Director Goes to Work	38
	Feedback as Guide for Management	40
VI	Person-to-Person Communication	42
	Conversations with Purpose	43
	More Than Telling and Listening	44
	When Prejudice is Encountered	45
	Listening as Communication	46
	Communication with Professionals	48
	Motivating Volunteers	49
	Dealing With Criticism	51
	Avoid Conversation Stoppers	52
VII	Making Telephoning Productive	55
	Provide Enough Phones	56
	Make Certain Phones are Covered	56
	Consider an Answering Service or Device	57
	Improve Staff's Telephone Techniques	57
	Management Action for Phoning Efficiency	59
	How to Make a Successful Telephone Call	61
	Keeping Telephone Costs in Line	63
	When to Telephone	64
	Phone Hints for Executives	65
VIII	Staff Meetings as Communication Medium	66
	When the Objective is Planning	67
	Brief Messages With One Purpose	69
	Executive Makes Staff Meetings Efficient	69
	Conferences for Monitoring and Feedback	70
	Staff Meetings for Problem Solving	72
	Calling Staff Conferences	73

Chapter	Title	Page
IX	The Spoken Message	74
	When You Invite Someone to Speak	75
	When You Are Asked to Speak	77
	Need a Speakers' Bureau?	79
X	Writing to Communicate	81
	Writing to Be Read Aloud	81
	Research and Preparation	84
	Writing to Be Read Silently	87
	Writing Persuasively	89
XI	Using Pictures for Impact	92
	Put Life in Your Illustrations	92
	Eliminate the Negative and the Distracting	94
	Focus on the Idea	95
	Captions That Capture Interest	95
	Using Pictures in Series	96
XII	High Priority Communication	99
	Assigning Communication Priorities	99
	Creating Unity of Board and Staff	100
	A New Trustee's Education	101
	Board Chairperson as Key Communicator	102
	Systematizing High Priority Communication	103
	Staff Reports and Reporting to the Board	104
	A Personal Touch in Fund Raising	105
	Handling Criticisms and Objections	106
	A Case of Incomplete Listening	107
	Dealing with High Priority Prejudice	108
	Communicating to Raise Money	108
	Direct Appeals and the United Way	110
	Selling Need for Overhead	111
	Keeping in Touch—A Lesson in Persistence	112
	Communication for Cultivation	113

Chapter	Title	Page
XIII	Building Good Relationships	114
	Maintaining Common Objectives	115
	Determining One's Publics	116
	Relations Are Everyone's Responsibility	117
	Enforcing the Rules—Three Case Histories	119
	Avoiding Distortion of the Message	120
	Sharing Objectives vs. Negotiation	122
XIV	Communication to Build Membership	127
	Building a List of Prospects	128
	Planning Membership Promotion Program	129
	Responding to Feedback	131
	Making the Program the Communication Medium	133
	Soliciting Memberships Personally	134
	Mystery of the Missing Members	135
	The Indispensable Telephone	135
	Acknowledging the Application	136
	Introducing the New Member	136
	Keeping Membership Communication Open	137
XV	Sell the Program	138
	Select the Targets	139
	Put a Plan Together	140
	Hints on Executing Promotion Plan	144
	Checklist for Program Promotion	146
XVI	Communicating Through the Annual Report	147
	Make the Annual Report Communicate	148
	Interpreting Statistics	149
	Dispelling Groupwork Myths	150
	Reporting Income Services	152
XVII	Keeping a Lid on Communication Costs	153
	Budgeting for Cost Control	154
	Economy Through Innovative Communication	155
	Cost Saving Case Histories	156

Chapter	Title	Page
XVIII	Communication in Action From Idea to Completion	158
XIX	PR Creates Low-Budget Revolution	165

CHAPTER I

COMMUNICATION --
ESSENTIAL MANAGEMENT INGREDIENT

Investigators once attempted to discover the personal characteristics which distinguished the highly successful executive. They examined histories, personalities, methods of managing and styles of America's highest-salaried chief executives. So varied were their findings that only two common, measurable characteristics emerged: **determination to succeed** and **large vocabulary.**

Based in part upon these findings a consensus has generally concluded that, to succeed in management, men or women must have clearly defined ideas of what they want to accomplish, knowledge and judgment to plan how, doggedness to stay with it until completed, and **ability to communicate their vision to others clearly and persuasively.** Whether written or verbal, skill in the use of the English language is the essential for every executive in finding out what he or she needs to know and in guiding others toward a pre-determined objective.

Communication is at the heart of every good management system. Upon how well an executive or manager communicates will depend employees' sense of direction and how fully they achieve the organization's objectives. This applies to programming and enlistment of clients and members, as well as broader-based community support. In the individual's own circumstance continuing communication with his or her governing board is vital to individual success and advancement also.

Skill in communicating varies widely although we have all been communicating since our first cry for mother's milk. One who is an excellent public speaker may be less able to express ideas persuasively in print or to build loyal personal relationships with associates. Study and training can greatly improve one's effectiveness in any aspect of communication.

Communication by Objective

In both private and governmental institutions, management has been developing increasingly effective systems and tools. A widely used system is management by objective (MBO). This method of making an organization work effectively has required superior performance in its communication functions. Whether a chief executive is directly responsible for communication operations or turns over portions of them to others, their part is vital. Communications activities provide the input—the creativeness, the ideas, the facts about needs and desires of the community the organization serves. They also comprise the output by which others become aware of the institution's objectives, goals and programs. In achieving MBO success an executive needs **communication by objective**, tightly controlled in respect to goals, time frames and monitoring, but flexible and creative as to methods.

Communication by objective organizes the public relations and internal relations functions as an essential part of the management process. It makes certain that every communication effort is directed toward the purposes of the organization as a whole. It avoids wasted effort on peripheral matters and concentrates on those which have higher priority. It can make the difference between uncertainty and clarity in management decision-making.

Under this system, communication does these things:

- Provides input from the community for defining long-range objectives.
- Obtains facts needed for determining intermediate goals.
- Defines work segments for accomplishment of goals.
- Monitors progress.
- Promotes programs and measures their success.

In practice communication by objective works this way. To determine the role of a social agency in community life, it must have well-developed lines of communication. These must answer questions about: patterns of services offered by other agencies; population makeup; expressed needs as determined by scientifically constructed surveys; evaluation of existing staff skills and facility resources; availability of volunteers and capacity to recruit, train and supervise them. From these answers, the board of directors and agency lay leadership can work together to construct long-range objectives that meet real needs and that can be defended as worthy of the community's support.

Second step is to determine short-range goals which will advance the institution toward the objectives already determined. Contrasting with five- and ten-year objectives, these goals may require from a month to a year for completion. Communication is between executive and staff, working together—and with outside expertise when necessary—to spell out programs by which agency objectives may be attained.

Third step in management by objective is to break down the tasks needed to reach the projected goals into job segments. These also are worked out by individual staff members with the executive. In turn, staff members define tasks to be performed by their volunteers and employees. The latter should assist with making these descriptions and agree they are within their capacity and willingness to accomplish.

Monitoring to see that tasks are accomplished **on time** is the responsibility of the executive and staff members. This requires maximum flow of information between persons accomplishing job segments and their supervisors. Monitoring is directed to two management requirements: knowledge of the quality of performance being achieved and of whether job segments are being completed on schedule.

If time segments allotted prove inadequate for any reason, it sends repercussions throughout the management system. This is avoided as good communication develops within an organization and as self-knowledge and understanding by staff of their own capabilities and time requirements grow.

Thus far communication's role has been internal in purpose—to provide policy-makers and management with knowledge needed for decision-making and planning and staff and volunteers opportunities for participation. The process has been two-way communication—information submitted and feedback returned. This is essential for management control. This two directional process continues in importance as communication moves from internal concerns and becomes promotional.

The fifth step for communication by objective is the point where many executives turn over responsibility to a communication professional. The communication specialist then plans a package of promotional activities to achieve management's requirements based on a specific program's appeal, previous experience with similar programs, the current climate for communication, and management's goals for applications and for time frames. The plan calls for deadlines for each communication segment—mailings, newspaper announcements, interviews over spoken media and talks before community groups.

Into each promotion effort are built targets—so many calls from listeners or so many application blanks returned. If promotion takes place over an extended time, weekly or monthly goals may be set: so many new memberships or clientele enrolled the first week, so many the second, and so on. This enables those in charge, when results fall short, to delve for reasons and to take any further actions indicated.

Tight monitoring of promotional results is equally important to management whether there is an over-response or a shortfall. In the former case, additional groups, leadership and supplies may need to be ordered. In the latter, additional promotion may be indicated—or a cutback in commitments to the project.

Management and Communication

Two conclusions emerge. Communication rates as one of topmost priority among management skills. And management of the communication process is as vital as in any other area of management responsibility.

A chief executive may feel more at home with the tangibles of productivity, programs and personnel than the more nebulous factors of media publicity. He or she can assign responsibility for the latter type of communication to others. He or she can also call for expert assistance in communication for fund raising. But, in the end, the person in charge cannot avoid ultimate responsibility for all communication. Upon it depends an organization's success or failure.

Communication by objective enables the executive to use and control communication in line with the institution's direction and purposes.

CHAPTER II

IMAGE-BUILDING--
A LONG-RANGE OBJECTIVE

An institution's image is what people believe it is—sometimes more or less than the truth. This has at times given "public image" a bad name as if it were something created to order by a Madison Avenue dream tank. Happy is the executive whose agency has a history of solid performance well-known to its constituency and no temptation to pretend to something it is not.

An image consists in large measure of reputation—a word in less vogue today than formerly. Over the years, the American Red Cross built a reputation for serving the victims of floods, hurricanes, wars and other disasters. This has been solidly based on massive relief and impressive statistics. But its image is something more—pictures which flash into the mind and cause warmth in the heart when Red Cross is mentioned.

The image of the American Red Cross is one of persons in action: The lovely poster girl in white nurse's uniform with red cross on cap or sleeve kneeling compassionately over a wounded soldier. Two olive-clad men in helmets carrying a man on a stretcher through bursting bombs. A gray lady calling on a service man's family.

Establishing an Ideal Image

By definition an image is a representation or reflection of the real thing. It develops from, and is created by, performance as that performance is communicated to others. It may, therefore, seem presumptuous to set an image as an objective. Yet without a sense of the organization's identity, its spokespersons have no guidelines.

One might have difficulty describing differences in the images of the Girl Scouts and the Camp Fire Girls. Yet one knows the differences are there, and one would sense something awry in a leader of the one who seemed rather to represent the outlook and attitudes of the other.

For this reason some organizations have chosen to adopt public relations platforms which, like platforms of political parties, state their purposes and principles. They also adopt guidelines for their communicators. Both should be approved at the policy-making level, and together they suggest the ideal image of the organization as envisioned by those responsible for its direction and continuing existence.

Most important is to have a platform or its equivalent written down. In the press of continuing operations, responsibilities and deadlines it is easy to forget the early vision and compromise with some need of the moment. Impressions also differ, especially in retrospect, and written documents save time and settle arguments when differences arise.

Institutional image as communication objective develops from an organization's central purpose and from other long-range objectives adopted by the board.

An organization's purpose may be individual development and character-building devoted to boys in their teens. If yours is a Boy Scout organization, you build an image through visible uniforms, community service, outdoor hikes and camping, courts of honor, merit badges, oath and scout laws. Your image objective is wide public awareness of adult-led youths, self-disciplined and serving the community.

If your organization is a YMCA, you build a different sort of image. Your objective is that of a less structured, more flexible organization serving older youth and adults as well. Your guidelines may call for a central building with facilities for swimming, basketball and other sports. You place emphasis on challenging ideas and training leadership. You also have camping and crafts, but without uniforms. You try to respond to community needs as they arise, but less conspicuously.

Both youth-serving organizations have strengths and weaknesses. But their images are different. With the scouts, there is less emphasis on buildings; troops often meet in churches or buildings of other sponsoring groups. But wherever scouts travel as units, their presence is recognized and by their actions they build an image of the scout movement. The "Y" by contrast tends to be identified with a building and its facilities. Its members are not easily recognizeable as such unless appearing in sports team uniforms. Communicating its mind-stimulating and spiritual-developing activities to a non-involved public is often a difficult task.

Guidelines Use With Fuzzy Image

Images of both these organizations have evolved over many years, and the local units take their cues from their national leadership and guidelines. The association which is without national affiliation and has been formed in response to a local need with no precedents to guide it may take months, even years, to develop a clear idea of the image it wants to acquire. Without precedents, disagreements arise.

In such an event a consensus on guidelines may avoid stalling of all public communication until complete agreement can be reached. For example:

A. Purpose of the Smithtown Civic Association is to promote pride in Smithtown and a community spirit which will slow down the exodus of its young people.

B. The Association will work with and support all other groups in their positive efforts to improve the community.

C. The Association will seek out and publish all strong points of Smithtown while encouraging and rallying support for every effort to remedy its weaknesses.

D. The Association will seek the cooperation of both print and air media in making the public aware of such efforts and of the schools in giving young people reasons for pride in their hometown.

These simple communication guidelines by-pass the arguments over whether the Association should seek an image as in the forefront of every effort for community advancement; whether priority should be given to environmental consideration or providing more employment. They enable the organization to assist the Garden Club in its effort to beautify the community with more flowers, trees and parks and the Chamber of Commerce's efforts to bring a new industry to Smithown. They provide movement toward its objectives without becoming controversial or deciding whether it is to be an organization out front or working behind the scenes.

The Value of a Symbol

Importance of an organizational image is more noticeable in large cities with many agencies serving community needs. There something distinctive is needed to stand out from the crowd. People tend to identify an institution by some visible aspect: "the club with the tennis courts," "the church with the white steeple," "the museum with the pillars." Or, they may think of it in connection with some service about which they hear a great deal—"the one that provides family counseling... has a senior citizens center...organizes the July 4th. celebration."

Building an image is comparatively easy for an organization with a single service—the Rescue Squad or the Visiting Nurses Association. The long-range objectives are specific and relative to volume and quality of service, not to serving a variety of needs. In both cases mentioned, the vehicles are identifiable— the ambulance by its appearance and flashing red light, and both by identifying names. Both win sympathetic attention by their observable members in uniform on errands of mercy.

But, an institution serving many types of persons and a variety of needs has a more difficult problem of projecting its image to the community whose support it requires. It may present several images as some persons become aware of one agency activity and others, of others. Or those who have little awareness of what it does may have very hazy ideas about it. The need is to make its image sharp and clear.

Fortunately for communication, most organizations begin with a simple purpose and a single program, later expanding to serve related or newly-observed needs. At such times it becomes imperative to change the organization's public image. This may be easier if the organization has developed a symbol.

Everyone is familiar with religious symbols—the star, the cross, the crescent—and most will be conscious of the YMCA's triangle and "Y", or the Boy Scouts' fleur-de lis and eagle. Such symbols develop from a process of stripping away the details and expressing the heart of one's reason for existence like the wheel chair symbol of one medical assistance association.

These symbols retain the loyalty and emotional involvement of people even when a cause has been lost or won. When, as an institution responds to new challenges, it becomes necessary to change an image, the task is easier if a symbol remains. When new tasks are not unrelated to, or inconsistent with, older ones, this merely means widening a symbol's meaning. The "Y" of YMCA comes to mean young in spirit instead of physically young as the organization expands its service from teenagers to middle-aged executive health clubs and The Old Guard for retirees.

How Does Your Image Rate?

A good image attracts people and resources. It is recognized within the community an organization serves. The community may be a geographical area or an economic or social grouping: a city, an ethnic group, the mentally disturbed, members of a profession or of a religious denomination. The question is: Within its community—and the wider community from which it draws financial support—does it have high or low visibility?

If, in a group of strangers, you remarked: "I am active with the Boy Scouts," chances are someone would at once remark, "Oh, yes, I know all about that organization." It would not matter whether the people actually were up to date with newer developments. A long history of conspicuous and popular activities of uniformed boys has made people conscious of Scouting's main thrust and purposes. They feel they know it.

On the other hand, if you were to state, "I am employed by the local Bureau of Social Service," there might be an awkward pause and visible expressions of puzzlement. The strangers may confuse the name with Social Security, a government activity; "Bureau" sounds like something official, although your agency may be privately supported. Or, some may have only vague ideas of what social service people do.

Does the Bureau help indigent families? Does it operate orphanages or old folks homes? Does it provide guidance counseling? Does it care for unwed mothers and arrange adoptions? It may do all these and more. But how does one convey this without thoroughly confusing people?

Goals for image building include:

1. Instant recognition. This is a primary goal whatever the agency's objectives. Lacking a symbol, one looks for some aspect of the organization which can be made visible and to which all communication can be related as starting point.

2. **Public approval.** The objectives of the institution must be related continually to the community's own purposes and the public good.

3. **Accepted as best among peers.** Every organization wants to deserve a reputation for quality performance. This calls for constant communication of successful efforts, also making the public aware of circumstances which at times make less than perfect performance necessary.

4. **Adjudged as sensitive to needs and concerned about people.**

5. **Evaluated as efficient and skillful custodians** of contributed resources.

6. **Personnel observed as capable and fair,** compassionate, but practical.

Creating an image based on such goals starts with the receptionist at the front entrance. Impressions of courtesy and consideration established by his or her attitude of helpfulness will be confirmed or weakened by every subsequent personal contact. Or impressions may begin with the telephone operator who answers a first call. Newspaper accounts, mailings, annual reports, program participation add to the picture an organization projects.

Publicity can be a two-edged sword. A reputation can be greatly enhanced by a single, dramatic, newsworthy event which shows the agency as successful. Also, it can be seriously damaged by a single conspicuous failure. Yet a reputation solidly built over many years will usually survive the sensational exception.

Most important is the image among the "in-group"—the core of leaders whose words to their friends will carry more weight than a published account by some unknown person. Thus it is important to recruit a governing board of men and women favorably known to many others in the community and volunteer leaders and participants whose involvement leads to enthusiastic comments in their outside relationships.

CHAPTER III

COMMUNICATION--
LIFEBLOOD OF AN ORGANIZATION

Without communication an organization dies.

An executive of a family service agency remarked:

"Unless I spend one-third of my time on the telephone, I'm not doing my job."

As successful executives know, constant communication provides the nourishment which gives an organization a sense of worth, direction and unity. It supplies the feedback information necessary for program planning and policy making. From the very beginning, it is the tool by which any organization is shaped and formed.

Every group starts with an idea. But, until the originator's conviction about its worth is communicated to others—until his, or her, own emotional commitment to it becomes contagious, nothing happens. Through discussion and criticism, the seminal idea is refined and amplified by incorporating suggestions of others until many people become involved and supportive. Thus an institution comes into being.

Communication, after making possible an organization's birth, continues as the means by which members of the group enlist others and generate continued growth. By communication its leaders are also able to measure its successes and failures with those it seeks to serve.

But growth changes things. The small, intimate institution, where everyone knew each other and everything that was going on, becomes a bureaucracy. The first fiery enthusiasm cools somewhat. The sense of unity—of **us together**—weakens as each individual becomes absorbed in his own area of concern. Feelings of competition and jealousy may arise as each unit has to justify its plans before being assigned a share of the total, but limited, resources. As an organization expands and takes on new tasks—its communication problems become more complex. In turn, its communication methods must grow more sophisticated and resourceful so as not to lose touch with its staff and clientele.

Communication Begins at the Center

In an established agency, communication starts with the chief executive. Like a wave from a pebble dropped in a pond, communication moves outward in orderly fashion, then returns as feedback bounced from the far shore of public opinion.

Communication must begin at the center because only the chief executive has in mind the total organizational picture. Only she or he can foresee all potential conflicts and prevent what may become disasters. The executive can delegate some communication responsibilities to a professional specialist or a capable, talented volunteer. But he or she can never escape major responsibility for all communication. Only the C.E. can veto an announcement based on some vested departmental interest when larger matters are at stake.

Because the chief executive is the only one with a complete picture, the governing board relies on him or her for guidance in policy-making. To its members the C.E. is the communication media by which clients directly or through staff make known their satisfaction or dissatisfaction with the organization's services. The C.E. collects and analyzes all information on the agency's performance and provides input in formal reports and personal contacts for board members' consideration.

Once policies and guidelines are adopted, it is the chief executive who passes them along to the staff, interprets them in the light of the board's discussions, and supervises their day-to-day implementation.

This is the ideal, of course, but consider what can happen when channels are not followed and communication is not cleared with the chief executive.

Snafu at the Youth Center

It is a lovely Saturday morning in September. The lobby is crowded with milling early-teen age boys waiting to register for the Youth Center's fall swimming classes. The harried receptionist has not heard about it—nor can she find it scheduled on the weekly list of events.

The receptionist tries telephoning the physical education director who is out jogging with the men's cardiac prevention group. His assistant is away with a weekend camping unit. A volunteer leader in charge of the calisthenics program answers the call. But he knows only that the pool is closed for its annual cleaning and repainting.

The chief executive's secretary does not come in on Saturdays, but the chief himself is finally located at a meeting. He says that re-opening of the pool has been delayed. The contractor is being held up by a slow delivery of a new part for the water pump. The original dates for registration and the pool's opening were never officially approved nor released. How could they have been leaked?

There is only one thing to do. The C.E. tells the receptionist to record the names, telephone numbers and addresses of all the boys and dismiss them with assurance they will be notified when new dates are set.

What went wrong with the communication program? Had some staff member who participated in the planning anticipated the announcement and passed the word without re-checking? Whatever happened, someone had by-passed the center and fouled up the communication process. Fortunately, most damage had been repaired by the C.E.'s prompt ordering of a new communication effort.

Thus, good communication begins at the center and expands first to those closest and most involved with the agency and its programs—the professional staff. Feedback at this point may well call for a pause for reflection. Without abandoning objectives, goals may need to be changed, timing extended, methods altered.

Enlarging the Information Circle

Once executive and staff have reached agreement, and implementation has been planned, the next step in communication is to involve the larger employee group. In this second circle from the center are persons like the receptionist in the snafu story who will have specific roles to play. Even those not directly involved may well be briefed so that they can answer questions from outsiders and share in the enthusiasm of staff members who planned the program.

In ever-widening circles information reaches the members, potential program participants, and finally, the general public.

Other "in-groups" will be notified early of developments touching their interest. These may include large financial supporters who have a special interest in a project—committee members, community leaders—when major developments are of concern to the community; and, where public tax funds are involved, key legislative and government officials.

The chief executive's task includes making certain that no person of importance to the institution is surprised by developments or embarrassed to learn first of such matters from an unofficial source. Often the C.E. by consulting them early may find their comments and guidance of help in enlisting essential support—especially with new projects.

Continuing Communication With Board is Vital

Once an organization's general purposes are established it becomes the responsibility of the governing body (Board of Trustees, Board of Directors, Board of Visitors—by whatever name it is called) to set policies and guidelines. It will also review and approve staff planning and programs to see that these follow established policies. Again the chief communicator is the administrative head who acts for the board as overseer and reports back to them on how things are working out. Any breakdown in this communication can lead to trouble.

Failure to brief some board members on staff planning and implementation may lead them to set off in some new direction in their thinking. This can result in revisions of policy in board meetings and waste of staff time devoted to preparation before the signals were changed. This is a hazard notably when new members join the board who possess pre-conceived notions of what the organization should be doing and without proper grounding in what it has already accomplished.

Unity within the organization, once goals have been established, should be a primary objective of all communication planning. Yet, to get everyone to look at the institution in the same light, to possess the same image of it and its objectives, is sometimes arduous. It is easier to straighten out staff members who arrive with an intent to "reform" an organization in line with their personal ideas than board members with similar motives. But unless differences are resolved at the board level, clear-cut directions cannot be given to the staff. The result is confusion. One executive's methods for handling such a problem are illustrated in the following case history.

Orientation for the New Trustee

The chief executive of a Jewish Community Center is having lunch with a newly-elected member of his Board of Trustees. The C.E. habitually calls and sets up an appointment during the first month after a trustee's election. From experience he has learned that this is essential before a trustee attends his or her first board meeting. At this time he briefs the newcomer on the center's history, principal objectives, present policies and future plans.

The administrator first sets about finding why his guest has consented to join the board. From past experience he knows some people join for social reasons; some for prestige because its members are leaders in the community; and others because of personal commitment to community service or to the cause which the organization represents.

Now and then, a new man or woman may have some hidden motive for which the C.E. probes. Perhaps it is a personal point of view she or he wants to "sell" to the board. Today's new member, it develops, is primarily interested in preserving Jewish cultural and religious heritage. He wants the center to hold classes on these for young people.

As the C.E. earlier explained to the author: "People don't read—at least, carefully. They develop mistaken ideas. Also it is difficult to get them together often for large meetings because of their other commitments—including the center's full schedule of programs. So I meet with them in small groups or individually. When they're available, I'm available—day or night. It's also easier to work things out that way.

"As a 'hired hand,' I can't speak out at board meetings and embarrass a member by telling him he's off-base. But, I train my chairpersons to be strong presiding officers and rule against matters which are out of order." This C.E. also briefs his chairpersons before each meeting. Because he is in continuing touch with all members personally and by telephone, he can often anticipate points of view which will emerge and pinpoint actions which are likely to be taken by others.

As today's meeting proceeds, the executive diplomatically tells his new member that the center's purpose is to provide recreational and social, not cultural, activities for the entire family—that is why people join it. Thus, the C.E. prevents the new member from making a potentially embarrassing **faux pas** at his first board meeting. And he saves the board from spending valuable meeting time to educate its new member. Gradually, as they talk, the new trustee comes to realize that his ideas do not fit into the organization's stated purposes.

Executives need to be particularly aware of board members who do not participate in meetings or respond to questions directed to them. Silence is feedback, too. While some women and men are naturally reserved, it is board members' responsibility to respond to proposals and bring their own evaluation to share with others. Thus silence becomes significant, perhaps ominous.

At times a member wishes to avoid stating his or her own opinion on a matter because of holding a strong view in opposition to a consensus of others. It may be that a proposal violates the trustee's ingrained prejudice—which he or she is reluctant to expose.

One member's lack of enthusiasm may be cause for delaying a matter until reasons for reservations can be privately explored. At times the non-supporter may have an important reason for objecting. It is then better to hold up a project until the hitherto overlooked aspect is fully explored or until the dissident individual catches up with the knowledge and enthusiasm of the others. Otherwise he, or she, may go along reluctantly— a cause for later regret. A well-trained chairperson will distinguish the genuine from the chronic objector and know whether to delay action or proceed.

Planning Is Essential to Communication Success

Following a board's policy decisions, communication takes on new dimensions. Transmittal of information to staff leaders and program planners comes first, then as programs are developed, to an ever-widening number of persons. With each step communication becomes less personal and may carry less impact. To make it effective, planning becomes essential.

Even with one-to-one interviews, forethought helps. But the more people a communication will reach, the more important is the advance planning. In each instance the communicator must ask himself, "What do I want to accomplish by this?" On the answer to that question will depend decisions on subject matter, method of presentation, media to be used. Depending on the persons to be reached, the media choice often seems endless: publicity, direct mail, newspaper notices, radio, television, postal card notices, bulletin board, house organ, newsletter, telephone calling group, and so on.

An executive tends to choose what best suits his own personal style. One who is an effective writer may do less well before a live audience. Some speakers can use audio-visual presentations dramatically—others only amuse their audiences by their ineptness—or put them to sleep. Every medium has its advantages and disadvantages for specific audiences, specific material and at specific times. Each requires some practiced knowledge and skill to use it most effectively. And in mass communication it is most important to provide for feedback.

Timing is one important aspect of planning. Communicators need to know the climate for a particular communication—whether groundwork has been laid for a particular statement, what will be the competition for the audience's attention. Sometimes it is important not to wait—but to issue a statement on a matter before rumors and false information set people's convictions about a matter in patterns which will be difficult to change.

Communication That Was Handicapped

In his book, "But Not in Our Block," Henry Viscardi, a dynamic leader in the movement for rehabilitation of the physically handicapped, recounts a tale of bitter opposition he once faced. His group had planned a training school for such unfortunates in a Long Island area. Having started in a garage in a nearby community, they already had a history of success and now needed room for expansion.

The group had located an area which needed upgrading. It planned a beautiful new building near a swampy dump. As its members viewed the matter, the school could only benefit its neighbors: It would upgrade the area and provide education to children unable to attend existing public schools, with savings to taxpayers.

Before plans were ready for an announcement, the news was leaked. People of the neighborhood spontaneously opposed the project. They viewed the school as something which could ruin their predominantly residential area. Passion, not compassion, ruled. They apparently envisioned cripples on crutches and in wheelchairs converging on their streets. Such constant reminders, as they imagined them, of what might happen to them at the next major highway crossing was more than they could accept. An appeal to their pride in having among them an institution which was already nationally famous was wasted effort.

This question must remain unanswered, but—might not the climate for communication have been quite different had the school people first shared their problems with the community and talked out mutual differences? We Americans have always resented elitist proposals, starting with our mother's command to "Drink the castor oil—it's good for you." Furthermore, those left out of the planning approach any proposal with different attitudes. They do not have the knowledge which the insiders have; they may not share the feeling of importance about the problem which those possess who have laboriously considered the alternatives.

Had Dr. Viscardi's people first publicized the problems of the handicapped—the lost production of people untrained, the enormous expense of rehabilitation and education to become self-supporting, tax-paying members of society—might not people have looked on the project more favorably? Would not the feedback of criticism by opponents have warned them to involve the people in a dialogue before bitterness took over?

Consider this communication strategy. Suppose the group had first proposed the building of such a school by public funds. In today's context, some people are claiming this as a responsibility of public education. Might not the specter of increased taxes to provide buildings which could accommodate wheelchairs and children on crutches have given way to sighs of relief at the revelation that it would be privately financed and supported?

Planning to Reach an Objective

Planning enables a communicator to do these things:

1. Establish objectives and ways of achieving them.
2. Set priorities so that major considerations are not over-

looked and neglected.

3. Eliminate irrelevant and unnecessary matters which distract an audience from the main point to be made.

4. Time announcements so that they do not compete for public attention. People find it difficult to absorb too much information at one time.

5. Provide a continuing flow of communications, giving an impression of a dynamic organization always doing something.

6. Reach a communication goal with maximum results and minimum expenditure of time and resources.

Spreading communications throughout the year also creates a better climate for the annual financial drive than sporadic announcements—or than merely reporting all achievements in the annual report at the end of the year, important as that document may be.

Planning a specific communication effort requires:

1. Stating the objective in such a way that it can be used later to determine whether the effort has been successful;

2. Dividing the task into work segments;

3. Charting the time frames for orderly work flow and coordination;

4. Assigning personnel and budget.

Let's say that the chief executive has indicated a goal of 200 senior citizens enrolled in your Monday courses and recreation program. From past experience you know that you will need at least 800 inquiries to generate that many enrollments. Your goal then is 800, not 200.

What will be needed to accomplish this? First step will be to prepare a prospect list or to decide how best your prospects can be reached. Fortunately, you have last year's enrollment list, prime prospects for this year. There will probably be a 20 percent attrition, however, so you will need new prospects just to remain even with last year.

You decide to get the list of residents in the new senior citizens housing complex—or failing that have leaflets distributed to every resident's door and posted on the bulletin board. Also, you will ask churches and service clubs to bring the program to the attention of their members. You make a note to inquire whether there is a local organization of retired people who might be willing to lend you its list of members. You give yourself a week to accomplish this step.

Next step will be a news release. It will need to contain all basic information about the program activities, eligibility requirements, and how to apply or to inquire further. You will need a brief radio version. You make a note to write the station program director with a suggestion that he might like to interview several of last year's participants on the air. You decide that the releases should go out a week in advance of any mailing and make a note for a follow-up release when returns begin to come in or just before closing date for applications.

Gradually you put together every step which will need to be taken with a deadline for its performance: preparation of mailings—writing copy, processing leaflets, letters, application forms, coordinating and inserting, post office delivery time. You assign target dates for the first responses and dates for achieving 25%, 50%, 75% and 100% of goal. Does it meet the closing date for applications?

When you have completed your plan, you call in your people who will do the processing and discuss your schedule with them. Can they perform in the time allotted? And will they reserve this time for this work? At this point you may have to make some adjustments.

Now you must check with whomever will process inquiries. Make certain they will keep on top of the recording and responding to potential applicants. You will need reports regularly both of inquiries and applications.

Plan also a backup strategy. What things can you do if the response is slow? Consider a telephone campaign. And don't overlook the possibility of urging those who have already enrolled to invite their friends to join them in attending.

At some time in the communication process, you may have to re-evaluate your plan. Perhaps you have over-estimated what you can do with your resources in a given time. Perhaps your goal is wrong—maybe you need 1,000 inquiries to generate 200 enrollments. Perhaps the original goals were unrealistic.

At any rate you must keep the chief executive informed of progress or lack of it. The C.E. must understand and approve your plan. If there is any reason to think it is not working, he must be notified at once so that he can revise his MBO plan. And the earlier, the better!

At each step in planning, you need to consult others whom

your plans affect. You need their judgment and insights. Moreover, you thus enlist their interest and enthusiasm. As the president of a large corporation once said, "You can hire the time of people, but you have to earn their interest and cooperation." You do this by sharing the fun of planning with them — and the responsibility and credit for making the plan succeed.

By letting employees and associates set their own evaluation of their capabilities, a manager challenges them to self-examination. One who asks himself or herself: "Is this my job, or your job?" and "How many bills am I capable of getting out in a day?" may well come up with more ambitious, but more realistic, estimates than the manager. He or she becomes "productivity conscious."

By thus enlisting others' creativity and expertise, a manager can make more accurate estimates of personnel needs. Of course, he or she will have constantly to re-evaluate the others' estimate and learn how capable they are at self-evaluation. By this program of consultation, an executive does not lose control of an organization. Rather, he or she manages a process by which an organization is created.

Consultation in this manner for communication by objective is somewhat like pulling, rather than pushing, a string through a hole. You surrender the authoritarian do-it-my-way method for the gentler, easier and often more effective method of challenging others to do their best.

CHAPTER IV

EXTERNAL COMMUNICATION -- GENERATOR OF COMMUNITY SUPPORT

Separation of internal and external communication is a matter of administration and methods, not of purpose. Every organization should speak with a single voice. As one experienced public relations specialist observed, "No company has been known to have a successful community relations program which has had poor employee relations."

Credibility and support of one organization urging more liberal treatment of labor foundered when its own staff protested its treatment of them. They demanded the same benefits the agency's spokesman advocated for those employed by others.

In this case there may have been a failure to distinguish between the "ideal" as the organization viewed it, and the reality of its own resources, in both external and internal communication. It suggests that every spokesman for an organization, whether volunteer leader or staff, should clear all statements with the chief executive, (or designated communications professional), who has the entire picture; otherwise efforts to become a public hero may appear to be hypocrisy to insiders.

Four Objectives of Communication

External communication has four major functions in support of an institution's purposes:

(1) To win community awareness and understanding of the institution's point of view;

(2) To establish rapport with those groups and individuals upon whose support its success depends;

(3) To enlist volunteer participation and financial support; and

(4) To promote its programs for social outreach and community betterment.

These functions, when stated in specific terms, may serve as broad communication objectives. A fifth function—feedback—has a different purpose. By determining and analyzing public reactions to an organization's statements and activities a communication specialist discovers reasons for failures. This serves as a guide for changing communication methods, or, when necessary, goals.

In the course of performing the first four functions, the communication specialist builds a public image for the institution and establishes a climate for future communications efforts. This activity is commonly referred to as public relations.

Improving the Communication Climate

Receptivity of people to an organization's message may depend on many things, some of them events beyond the control of the organization itself. People may be preoccupied with other matters which seem more important or more pressing. Or, they may for good reasons or bad ones be prejudiced against, or unreceptive to, any change of the kind advocated.

Overcoming such obstacles may require long years of continuing education and discussion, or waiting for a turn of events which dramatize a problem and make people receptive to solutions.

Two things an organization can do to improve its climate for communicating are:

• Build an image for accuracy, honesty, reliability and reasonableness in its communication, and, in its actions, for dedication to society's welfare, sensitiveness to individuals' needs, ability to get things done, accountability for stewardship of public contributions.

Such an image built on solid performance and on communication of that performance to others establishes the right to be heard and considered whenever it has something to say. It is axiomatic that once an individual or institution has been spotlighted in the news its subsequent activities become of interest to the reading public, therefore more newsworthy. It becomes easier to obtain attention in newspapers and other media.

• Establish good mutual relationships with all groups and

persons who comprise the institution's natural constituency and with others whose support will be important to its success. In the latter group should be included suppliers and service organizations—for example, commercial organizations such as printers whose performance on time may be critical in a promotional mailing.

Good communication and good relations over a long term enable your supporters to give you the benefit of doubt when you stumble, or some turn of events not of your making seems to weaken your cause. Good relations in the past provide a favorable climate for dialogue in the present if differences arise.

Building an Image Is Endless Task

Every public institution has a public image. This image may be different with different people according to what exposure they have had to its personnel and activities. A major objective of communication should be to create a single image such as the governing board has envisioned.

Of course, some agencies have better communication than performance. An unjustified reputation with the public causes those in position to know better to speak of them cynically. Unless they are quickly able to make their actions catch up with their promises, they stand to lose in public esteem. Once people perceive an image as false, it is hard to regain their confidence.

For this reason, it may be desirable to present the organization as a dynamic institution, working toward a desirable image, changing in response to changing situations—not one which has already attained standing. This can have a strong appeal to public sympathy. President Franklin D. Roosevelt gained great public support when he said he would promise no miracles but would try hard to solve problems of the great depression.

When achieved, the public image of an agency performing a great community service, responding to perceived needs, consistent in its announcements and concerned about people becomes a valuable asset. Its statements are accepted less critically. People want to work for it—whether as paid staff or volunteers. They can readily agree with its objectives and proudly support its efforts. Financial supporters feel that their contributions will be well spent.

The public and insiders need to share this image. Each needs continually to reinforce the other in the rightness of their judgement and faith in the institution. It is reassuring to people to know their friends and acquaintances confirm their view of the organization's merit.

A solid public image serves well also when a crisis comes. At camp there may be a disaster of a youngster injured or an epidemic of disease. Someone may have erred, or the incident may have been beyond the institution's control. In either event, the agency's friends will adopt a wait-and-see attitude and, considering past service, more readily forgive an error of judgment. Professionals like to cite the fact that the standing of President Eisenhower in the U-2 incident and President Kennedy in the Bay of Pigs matter actually increased in opinion polls after they admitted their errors. This underscores the need for honesty and accuracy in communication even when it can tarnish the image one has worked long and hard to build.

Society changes, and institutions must change in order to survive. An agency succeeds in the purpose for which it was formed. Should it go out of business or tackle some new and related problem? Society changes its priorities as events call attention to inequities previously overlooked, making an agency's main objective obsolete. We have seen this in the "discovery" of sex and racial discrimination, ecological damage, energy problems and poverty. Although national in scope, they affect every community. Agencies which serve locally must take these newer preoccupations into account.

Agencies for developing leadership qualities in boys have found they must include girls. Ones founded to serve middle income youths have extended their services to the inner city underprivileged. Organizations which once helped rural homemakers, now teach nutrition in the "ghettoes." All such agencies have revised their images.

Organizations holding rigidly to old objectives often find their images are tarnished and their support weakened. By contrast, some others, in changing, reduce their standards and lose their sense of direction. Consider the following.

Case of Lost Identity

Philadelphia's Girard College is an example of an institution which, in changing, for a time lost its sense of identity. Founded under the will of Stephen Girard, a Frenchman who emigrated to America in colonial days, the college was a residence school for orphan boys.

Girard had observed a need for education and training of the sons of widows left indigent by the untimely death of their husbands. By his direction the school's objective was to make its students self-supporting in a trade by age eighteen. To this end, admission standards were strict, teachers able, and discipline tight. A student's time was so structured with classes, studies, sports, and other extra-curricular activities that he had little time for mischief. Neatness in grooming, dress and conduct were required.

Applicants for admission were plentiful at first. The college took only younger boys. Through the years, with other institutions serving the same need and with more affluent families, applications decreased. Requirements for admission were eased as to residence, age, and family circumstances; ethnic restrictions were removed.

Yet applications failed to increase. One reason was relaxation of discipline—easing of standards for appearance and deportment. An attitude of permissiveness led to loss of morale, weakening of faculty, and eventually closing of some school buildings.

Alumni expressed their concern to no avail. It took a lawsuit by an aroused parent demanding compliance with terms of the Girard will to turn the school around. Loss of a sense of identity had nearly destroyed the institution. Now an effort is afoot to recapture the school's self-image. Communication with alumni has been restored. Girard seeks to tighten its standards and again become a useful institution in contemporary society.

This illustrates the dangers of failure to adopt new objectives and to revise the ideal image for which an organization strives —or to restate them in a new context. As a contrasting example of positive action, consider the experience of what is now known as the National Foundation. Its transformation can provide inspiration for communication planning.

Foundation's Face-Lifting

One bright spot in the Great Depression era was the launching of the March of Dimes. It had a visible symbol of its fight against the crippling disease of polio in the President of the United States who had himself overcome its ravages. Franklin

D. Roosevelt was an inspiration to all others similarly victimized. The appeal for millions of small donations, providing a popular base of support, was possible because of mass media exposure.

The National Foundation for Infantile Paralysis attacked the polio problem on two fronts: research to remove the dreaded danger and help for its victims until that goal could be realized. Funds for prosthetic devices and rehabilitation were supplied for administration by local chapters in counties across the nation. With highest-level backing, this non-profit enterprise grew in prestige comparable with the long-established and equally non-partisan American Red Cross.

Eventually its grants to research scientists resulted in a break-through—the discovery of polio vaccines. What should an organization do under such circumstances? Announce its victory, and go out of business? In the minds of many persons, it had proved too valuable an institution for solving health problems for that.

Instead, its policy makers dropped the limiting phrase from its name and stated purposes, and it became the National Foundation. It broadened its area of concerns to include other diseases. It remains a viable institution—less visibly dynamic and broadly supported perhaps, but still an institution with a solid reputation for performing a service.

From the National Foundation's experience several things are noticeable. One is the relative ease of communicating with people about a single, dramatic objective. In its early days, the Foundation presented itself in exciting ways. There was the annual poster boy or girl on crutches or in a wheelchair; a White House reception for the youngster selected for this honor; both were widely reported in the media. Few people could refuse the once-a-year appeal for a modest contribution to help children such as these.

A second lesson is that, once public understanding of a problem has been achieved, future communications can be simplified. A child in a wheelchair or on crutches became almost a trade mark for the Foundation and its work.

A third lesson is that when an organization takes on new, additional objectives its image becomes less clear—the impact of its communications on people's consciousness becomes scattered and less distinct. It takes extra effort to communicate effectively.

For example, a local YMCA was organized many years ago to provide the community with health-building recreational facilities and mind-stimulating discussion groups in a religiously-oriented atmosphere. Today it has become a community asset which is hard to describe in a few words. It has responded to community needs by training industrial supervisors in human relations and in sensitiveness to individual differences; by developing leadership skills in teen-age boys and girls; by extending learning efforts in crafts to underprivileged ethnic youngsters; by providing a meeting ground for threshing out ethnic differences.

Such an image is difficult to project except over a long period of time. Even then, not all persons will view the organization in the same light. Briefing volunteers who solicit financial contributions has become an extensive and, in some ways, difficult task.

Steps for Building an Institutional Image

To create a favorable public image of itself, an organization should:

- Adopt clearly-defined purposes, stated in writing and approved by the governing board.
- Agree on specific long- and short-range objectives for achieving those purposes.
- Plan, at executive level in consultation with staff, a strategy for reaching the objectives.
- Establish deadlines for reporting progress and any difficulties encountered.
- Determine channels for clearing program announcements and other communication, for reporting statistics and their evaluation.
- Provide methods of keeping board members informed of progress between meetings.
- Execute communication actions for building understanding of problems and points of view and support for programs with both interested groups and general public.

- Time communication efforts from center outward—beginning with those who are directly responsible for carrying out programs and including others in accordance with their interest and need to know.

- Break down each communication effort into individual tasks, assigning to each its time frame, essential personnel and money resources, choosing media, methods and message content.

- Assign measurable target results to every communication task. These should be determined by proper goals and reasonable expectations. They will later serve for evaluation.

- Build feedback into every communication program, or arrange for other means of testing public reactions.

- Assign monitoring responsibilities to determine whether targets are being met as the program proceeds.

- Adjust or augment original communication plans as need is determined. Correct misimpressions or deviations from objectives before a wrong image becomes fixed in people's minds.

Such organization of effort will present an image of an institution which knows what it wants to accomplish and how to accomplish it, which conserves its efforts for the main purpose instead of being tempted into side issues or perhaps lesser, but more pressing problems.

Keeping Image Current

In an era of change, keeping constituents up-to-date on changes affecting the organization and its responses to these changes can be a continual struggle. People need to know about the problems before they learn about programs designed to meet the problems.

Timing is important here because, if constituents first learn about the programs and restructuring of personnel and resources to cope with new problems, they may resent them. Without a feeling for the importance of some new problem, they retain an emotional investment in programs they have already supported. They see the new programs as competitors with the objectives and programs which they have previously been "sold."

An example is the experience of many colleges and universities with their alumni during the 1960s. Because they had not informed their alumni of the changing nature of student bodies and the need to respond to black students' demands, the former graduates were unprepared for what happened. To nostalgic alumni, student violence was an attack against the **alma mater** they held dear. In male institutions the demand for admission of women was also a rude shock; and students' demands for representation on college governing bodies seemed impertinence to alumni who looked upon such election as a crowning lifetime honor.

For alumni and alumnae of U.S. higher institutions of learning, the fractured image of a favorite institution was too heavy a burden to bear. Many withdrew their financial support. Some independent colleges have succeeded in repairing their images and gaining back much expected support; others already struggling with heavy burdens appear to have been dealt mortal blows. Had they kept current their communication of problems, as well as achievements, alumni might have rallied to the support of what they perceived as dynamic institutions responding to new needs, aware and in control of the social currents effecting their destinies.

Communicating New Problems

New—or newly perceived problems need to be presented in context and dramatized with personal examples. Movements of blacks and other ethnic people into white suburban neighborhoods has been violently resisted in some areas. In one metropolitan community the newspaper was persuaded to publish a long article with family pictures about one black professional couple's difficulty in locating suitable housing. Many white readers must have blushed with embarrassment. Not long afterward blacks began to purchase homes and move into the area quietly and without open criticism.

Statements of new problems should, whenever possible, show how they grow out of old problems. In the present-day context of de-emphasis of sex stereotyping and female progress toward equality, opening of a boy's school to co-education can be shown as a natural evolution. If the school's original purpose was development of mature character in boys, association with female peers may be perceived as a necessary and natural part of their education. A brief for co-education may be based on the premise that both family and business life will be improved if the sexes are not segregated in their teens. Attitudes toward the opposite sex may be healthier if based on reality rather than fantasies.

A word of caution about this approach is in order. One institution in adopting this philosophy toward admission of blacks encountered an adverse reaction. Black students came to feel that they were doing the white students a favor by their presence. They did not look upon the mixing of races as an educational advantage for blacks as well as whites. **Mutual benefit needs stressing no matter for whom the communication is primarily prepared.**

Another guideline for getting constituents to welcome a new challenge is to emphasize the positive. The President's Committee for Employment of the Physically Handicapped achieved spectacular results over many years by this approach. By emphasizing what handicapped people **could** do at work the Committee was able to sell the concept that "When properly placed on a job, a person's handicap is irrelevant."

Avoiding an approach which had failed in European countries based on special concessions and quotas, the Committee gained wide acceptance of the handicapped on a competitive basis. They induced employers to accept them for their accomplishments, not reject them for their disabilities. In some cases they were able to point to handicaps as advantages: deafness in high level noise areas, smallness in confined work areas, blindness in darkrooms, inability to walk in operating a telephone switchboard.

The Committee succeeded in selling industry on removal of many unnecessary job restrictions which discriminated against the physically handicapped. It is now applying the same approach to the mentally retarded and mentally restored. Long before equal employment opportunity became a national policy, astute leaders gained entry of black men and women into the business community by a similar approach. Many preconceptions and prejudices disappear before reasoned appeals and continuing factual stress of the positive.

Keep the Information Flowing

A forward planning specialist for a major business company once observed, "Outfits which fail to **continually** make small changes will eventually undergo a revolution."

The same is true of communication. Failure to keep constituents abreast of small changes leads to a need for a major communication effort as colleges learned in the 1960s. People can absorb and accept only so much information at any one time. A flow, not a flood, is the ideal. If they do not receive information during the year, they are unlikely to catch up when the annual report arrives.

Continuous flow of information via many media also helps build an image of an organization which is on the job the year around, alert to problems and needs, not one feverishly active to catch up with itself when time for the annual drive approaches. This tends to project the kind of image which gives constituents confidence in continuing to support an organization with their time and money.

CHAPTER V

DELEGATING COMMUNICATION RESPONSIBILITIES

Although a chief executive cannot in theory avoid ultimate responsibility for communication, practical considerations usually require the delegation of much of the actual work to others. Limitations of time and energy suggest most organizations require someone whose entire, or at least major, attention is given to communication problems if they are not to be neglected.

A C.E. may well wish for an **alter ego**—someone as knowledgeable, someone who thinks and acts the same as he or she would, were there time and inclination. On the other hand a C.E. who is skilled only in certain areas of communication may look for someone who complements his or her own abilities.

Many agency executives appear to feel more confident in dealing with internal communication. They are perhaps more at home with matters of programs, personnel and finances than with public relations. The former seem more concrete and measurable, more easily subject to judgment and control. They seek public relations specialists.

Other C.E.'s who enjoy speaking, interviews and public contacts assume the role of spokesman, leaving some reliable associate to direct internal communication and operations. In this event some staff person will have to assume the detail work of public communications implementation.

An ideal arrangement in an agency of modest size is often for the board chairman as head of the policy-making body to be the spokesperson on all major matters, the C.E. as administrator to handle internal communication, and a specialist to direct public relations in accordance with the C.E.'s management-by-objective plan. Of course, individual talents and convenience will, at times, dictate departure from such rigid lines, but with clearances by those concerned.

Picking a Public Relations Person

Before selecting someone to direct an agency's communication with the public, a chief executive will do well to consider his specific situation. Are the problems of communication simple and limited in scope—or complex and sophisticated? Is the organization's story easy to tell, or does it involve many types of service to the community? Are the available media and methods of telling the story few in number, or is there a wide choice calling for much knowledge and judgment? Is there much competition for media attention? Will the media be sympathetic and helpful?

Other questions sharpen this analysis. Who are the people whose support the agency needs? Where are they to be found and how reached? The answers may suggest selecting a person of one type rather than another.

A small agency with a small budget in a small community with a single newspaper and one "coffee-pot" radio station may need little help. The answer may be a part-time man or woman reporter or a correspondent for out-of-town papers. Or, perhaps the agency will look for a volunteer—a retiree or homemaker seeking an outlet for his or her talents and a chance to be of service.

In such a person, a most important quality to look for is **ability to communicate**. This is not necessarily the "A" student in English composition, although ability to write clear, understandable copy is essential. More likely prospects may possibly be found among good writers of inter-office memos at work, or someone who has edited a high school newspaper or church bulletin. Their interest is not in pride of authorship or style, but in getting the message across.

The small agency may well find that its public communication problem calls for a different approach. Perhaps the chief solution may be someone who can speak before group meetings of potentially interested people, or call individually on prospective members and supporters to explain the organization's purpose and benefits. This would be especially appropriate where an idea is complex and new. Then one would look for a verbal, sales-type person, rather than one skilled at writing.

In a city environment, and especially in a large organization with many services to describe, a person more sophisticated in communication will be required. Here college graduates of journalism and public relations courses offer advantages. One would be preferred who has had experience working with the media and knows the requirements—and perhaps the key personnel—of newspapers, radio, television, magazines, house organs and the like.

Such a person also knows the importance of accuracy in details, how to condense material for public service announcements on the air, the method of constructing a news story with its lead paragraph answering the questions of who, what, when, where, why and how?

Another asset is a "nose" for news and human interest. A good publicist is not content with the routine story covering the facts, but looks for the incident or example which illustrates a point. Always alert to the things editors are seeking, such a person knows that photographs of animals always attract reader attention and that what comes naturally to children always interests adults.

Sensitivity to interests and needs of readership and audience is important in a communicator, and especially in a social agency. In communication-by-objective this becomes an asset in monitoring communication results and in adjusting communication strategy which stumbles.

In searching for a public relations director, a C.E. may hope for someone who covers the broad field of communication; who is skilled in both written and spoken language, acquainted with key media persons, knowledgeable in social problems, dedicated, careful and accurate in research and statements, self-effacing; and who possesses good judgment. Most executives will settle for something less.

Orientation of the New PR Person

Practice of public relations is conducted on two levels: long-range and short-range. Both executives and PR professionals tend to reverse priorities in action—to take care of immediate, pressing matters and neglect things vital to an organization's future. Among the latter are public relations planning, setting down specific objectives for programs in writing, and periodic evaluation.

For this reason, it is important to anyone on a new major PR assignment to take time before getting involved in day-to-day operations to gain perspective on what she or he is expected to accomplish.

Soon enough you will become preoccupied with writing copy, telephoning, clearing releases, making press contacts, arranging for appearances on radio and television, setting up meetings, and a multitude of other details. As someone has said, "When you are up to your knees in alligators, it is hard to remember that you came to lower the dam."

With a mind still uncluttered by urgent pressure to do something about an appeal for more camp scholarships or arranging a meeting date for the PR advisory committee, the new PR person should:

- Acquire a thorough knowledge of the Board's policies and objectives, and of the agency's 1-, 5- and 10-year goals.

- Acquaint himself or herself with all key personnel, including directors of programs, and learn their ideas of how PR activities could help make them more successful.

- Learn to know what groups are the agencies "publics"— its staff, employees, volunteer leaders, program participants, beneficiaries and financial supporters—meet a representative sampling in order to be able to envision with whom he or she will be communicating.

- Discover what variety of communication media are available and meet their editors who will pass judgment on news from the agency.

- Record this information for convenient reference.

- Define the communication assignment as he/she understands it and have it approved in writing by the chief executive.

Planning PR Program and Setting Priorities

In collecting information about the job to be done, a new PR person may find it astute to make memoranda of each person met and to keep a file of them on 3 x 5 cards. Arranged alphabetically, with full name, address, phone number and some detail which serves as memory reference, they can prove a valuable resource and time-saver.

Objectives and policies are essential for ready reference. If not already available in printed form, it could be valuable for the director to write a PR platform based on an understanding of these and submit it for revision or approval. Guidelines of this nature and a description of the image toward which the organization is striving become valued reference points and save much checking with the C.E.

Next step is for the PR director to plan his or her communication and other activities in support of the organization's objectives. This requires a suggestion of what will be necessary in the year ahead in the way of mailings, releases, and the like with a conscientious estimate of money and person-power needed. At the same time it is desirable (although it may be too early to do so), to estimate goals in the way of responses to mailings or announcements. This is so that the administration can grasp what it is buying.

This planning should be thoroughly reviewed by the C.E. who should also assign priorities and with whom time frames should be worked out.

With such a road map in hand, the conscientious PR-person need not later be pressured into devoting major time to one department head who demands it—to the neglect of perhaps more modest claimants with projects more important to the agency's future.

Once a PR-director has set goals in increased membership, or larger financial donations, for example, there is a means for checking the success of a communication task. Goals should be stated in definite numbers, percentages, dollars or other measurable figures. In some instances, it may be necessary to take an informal survey to provide a base with which to measure such less tangibles as increased support for, or decreased opposition to, an institution's point of view on an issue—or public awareness of some agency activity. Where necessary, this should be done as early as possible. It might be accomplished by telephoning every tenth name in the phone book or by a double-postal questionnaire mailed to a cross section of an important group.

With a plan such as this for communication by objective in support of the organization's stated goals, the PR director has the best possible instrument for justifying his communication activities. In the minds of the C.E. and of hard-headed members of the board, communication expenditures are shown to be productive and justified.

As communication is vital to management, so this kind of management is invaluable to communicators. At best, PR activities are supportive of goals set by others. For this reason, PR persons can never take all the credit, nor should they receive all the blame. Some goals will be reached, others not. Communication is still an inexact science like weather predicting. But communication-by-objective provides a handle to grasp and removes some guesswork. It gives the PR-person reason for greater confidence and professional self-respect.

The PR Director Goes to Work

Preparations completed, the PR director turns to the problem with first priority. Perhaps it is promotion for the summer camp. Steps to take are:

1. Research. Collect all pertinent facts including background of previous camp seasons; dates, courses, activities, facilities, personnel and their qualifications, location and how to get there, advantages of attending, costs, requirements for admission, pictures from past years, case histories of campers, and third person testimony such as awards, recognitions and letters from parents.

2. Statement. From the collected material prepare a basic document containing all the information available and check with the director and others in charge for errors or omissions. From this document, information will be drawn for all oral and written communications about the camp. It will serve as ready reference for information operator and others in answering inquiries. From it will be drawn material for press releases, promotional folder, slide film, proposals for newspaper features, radio interviews and group talks.

3. Prospects. Identify people on whose interest and support the camp's success depends: youths, parents, potential contributors of camperships.

4. Media. Decide most effective methods for getting your message about camp to these groups. Note deadlines for copy to editors and printers, calculating backward from target date for publication and mailing. Allow extra time to accommodate unforeseen accidents and holdups. Allow time for photographic processing.

5. **Copy and layout.** Select photographs. Write text and captions. Keep in mind at every point the nature of the people with whom you are communicating. Boys, girls, parents, donors will have different interests and need different types of approaches. Yet, a son's mother may read over his shoulder, so don't go overboard on the hazards of canoe-jousting. Communication plan may include a general radio interview, a slide film, a letter, a folder, publicity releases. Adapt writing style to the specific media's requirements. Include all essential information, especially how to apply or to obtain more information.

6. **Targeting.** Note closing date for reception of applications in order to make proper preparations. Set goals for numbers of applicants—with intermediate goals, such as two weeks before, four weeks before, the closing date. Assign targets for inquiries in response to each communication effort with check dates for monitoring progress.

7. **Feedback.** Provide encouragement for feedback with each promotional communication: application blank, information coupon, address to write, phone number to call, return card. Build in a sense of some urgency to action providing for a noncommittal response. Deadlines or the possibility that not all candidates may be taken move people to respond promptly before their interest is diverted. "First come, first served" has long been such an incentive. Noncommittal responses, such as inquiries for more information, enable you to put the writers on a prospect list for follow up, by phoning, if necessary. In some cases advertising may be needed where editors fail to include how-to-apply information in news stories.

8. **Coordination.** Check with whoever is assigned to keep a record of inquiries that provision is made not only for recording the numbers of inquiries and applications, but also the names and addresses of every prospect with telephone number for rechecking as final deadline approaches.

9. **Monitoring.** No PR director can turn a communication effort over to others and forget it. One must follow through to see that instructions are carried out and that results are as expected. A chart with target dates X-ed out as completed helps a PR director keep a visual image of work accomplishments and work still to be done. On each check date it is necessary to ob-

serve whether results are satisfactory and to report to management.

10. **Consult and revise.** One of the most important of communications is reporting to the chief executive. Without conscientious reporting by subordinates, a C.E. "flies blind" and may be the last to know when grandiose schemes are doomed to failure. Whether news is good or bad, early advice and consultation enables a C.E. and PR director to decide whether to step up or step down communication efforts, or whether the project needs to be abandoned for lack of interest.

Feedback as Guide for Management

Management of an agency and management of its communication with the public must both rely heavily on feedback as a guide to success. Relationships with outside groups are built upon mutuality and understanding of the other's point of view. It is possible by discussion and inquiry to learn other groups' outlook in general. But to know the others' attitude fully it is necessary to observe individuals' reactions to something specific.

For this reason, feedback is invaluable. We know that parents generally welcome an opportunity to send their boys and girls to well-managed camps with character-developing and skill-training objectives. We know that, in general, they feel this is desirable and worth while. But how deep is that conviction? Will it, in their minds, over-balance the value of a family vacation together? In a tight economy will they sacrifice some desire of their own to send Johnny or Susy to camp? Not until a specific offering is made will you know.

When a mail offering of day camp for pre-schoolers fails to bring an anticipated response, it is important to find out why at once. Has there been some flaw in the communication—some vital information omitted? Or, is the climate wrong for this type of offering now? Is it a matter of money and should an installment plan be offered? Is timing off, or should the project be abandoned? Perhaps the wrong group was selected for the offering, and another mailing to another group may be indicated? Would a few telephone calls to prospects chosen at random provide an answer?

Sometimes a rumor, mis-information or the skepticism of some key person will kill all chances for success. The sooner one learns this and discovers how to handle the situation, the better for the agency and all concerned.

CHAPTER VI

PERSON-TO-PERSON COMMUNICATION

There's a fatal temptation for those who use mass media such as motion pictures, television, radio and the wire services.

There's a sense of power in sheer numbers which lets them forget that those numbers represent individual people. This is especially true for those who deal with advertising and the purchase of an audience of so many millions.

Even audience surveys of readers' or listeners' attitudes somehow homogenize the communicator's input so that he or she accepts unquestioningly the 60% favorable response, forgetting the 30 percent negative attitudes and the 10 percent who could not care less. People change attitudes with exposure. Songs, television programs and plays which achieve overnight success sometimes fail to last a week as wider exposure reveals flaws the adverse critics were first to notice.

For this and other reasons, there is no substitute for direct personal discussion for true understanding. All other forms of communication are substitutes and compromises because of the limitations of time, money, distance. It is more economical to address a large audience than to talk to a single person, or to telephone than to travel to see someone, or to notify a million people of something by an advertisement in a magazine than to send each a postal card. Yet, each medium or method has its disadvantages for which one must compensate in order to communicate effectively.

In order to do this, communicators need to understand face-to-face, person-to-person communication thoroughly and to be aware of differences when they use other ways. In such a personal discussion or confrontation, you are aware of voice inflections, facial expressions, body language. You are close enough in one-to-one conversation to sense what the other is feeling but not saying. You can better judge sincerity, defensiveness, fear, anger, boredom, distraction.

Face to face, you can rather accurately decide whether the other has heard and understood what you have been saying. You have an immediate response and may get an immediate decision, even if it is a decision to delay a decision.

Compromises in using other communication methods are often obvious. You shout to be heard at a distance. You speak more slowly with emphasis and gestures when addressing an audience. You use more descriptive phrases and voice inflections on the telephone to compensate for what the other cannot see. You feel compelled to organize your material better when writing a letter or using other means where people are no longer a captive audience.

With mass media, you dramatize and get quickly to the point to capture and hold attention. You use attention-compellers, wit, a photograph, a teaser to capture and hold interest while you lead into the message which is important to you.

Conversations with Purpose

To make a conversation successful, thought and planning come first. Otherwise, one may find at the end that, far from selling a point of view to someone else, one has for lack of evidence or reasoning accepted the other's outlook.

One would not keep an appointment for a job interview without not only planning and rehearsing what one wants to say, but also trying to anticipate hard questions and objections and preparing to handle them. Often one rehearses what one plans to say with a friend whose judgment is of value, accepts criticism, then changes strategy. (In contrast, at work too often one gives way to an emotional reaction to pressures and pours out one's frustrations without anticipating where this will lead!)

Before an important discussion, first decide what you would like to come out of the conversation—agreement, a decision, a promise of support or cooperation. Plan to talk in specifics, not generalities which might lead to misunderstanding.

Next plan to listen, as well as talk. An appearance of a closed mind, a bruised ego, or self-serving is self-defeating. Ask yourself: Am I prepared psychologically? Am I open to ideas and suggestions—whatever I may hear? Am I ready to probe beyond the other's words to find out what he or she really means? People sometimes say "Yes" when they mean "No" because they do not want to offend or embarrass another. But they are more apt to be open to your ideas when they sense you are really trying to understand and weigh their points of view. You can help by re-stating what the other has said in your own words, "You mean so-and-so?" In considering the way you put it, they may clarify a point in their own minds while trying to make it clear to you.

Perhaps you are discussing a job assignment with an employee. Although you know how you would like to have a conversation go, don't expect it to follow your course. The point is not what you **tell** the other, but what you both **agree** upon. You can hire bodies to fill openings in the work force; what you really want is understanding, total abilities and a will to use them toward achieving goals in assigned tasks. In short you want loyal, enthusiastic, dedicated workers. You cannot earn this by restricting their participation, but rather by enlarging their involvement so that the organization's goals and your goals become theirs as well.

One point to remember is that ideas are bought, not sold. When another does not completely accept a proposal, it is important to find out why. He or she may have a point. Or, sometimes your way of stating something has no real meaning for another until re-stated in his or her own words or from her/his point of view. Ask how he/she would state it, and sometimes a face will light up with sudden recognition—or you may find you must try again to make a matter clear. The point is to keep the conversation going until there is some base of understanding and the climate is favorable for presenting new evidence.

More Than Telling and Listening

To reach complete understanding, more than telling and listening is needed. One must be completely aware of the other person, to observe facial expressions and body language, to assess whether or not the other is telling the truth. Observations of involuntary gestures may not always be taken literally as indicated in texts on how to read people, but they are clues. Total impressions can provide a warning of something to examine further or to question.

By giving someone your complete attention you not only are better able to judge progress and keep control of the conversation, you also flatter the other's ego and make him or her more receptive to your own suggestions.

If one has decided in advance what one would like to produce from an interview, one can better keep the conversation from wandering or get it back on the track with a verbal nudge or a question. If one runs into opposition, one can plant seeds for thought and adjourn the matter until another time when the other person may be more favorable to suggestions. If one fails to have such an objective, one may come away accepting the other's viewpoint by default.

When Prejudice is Encountered

Everyone likes to think that his or her actions are based on reasoned judgment. But most of us are at times subject to prejudices. These may be convictions based on experiences of a lifetime which seem to us to make them indisputable facts. When we hear someone praised who has treated us shabbily, or nilified who has been honest in dealing with us, our first reaction is outrage.

Yet we know some people are two-faced. What bothers us is that, if the other's statements are true, our faith and sense of security in a relationship are not soundly based. We also tend to resent people from other cultures and backgrounds in proportion to the threat they seem to pose to our own. But much prejudice is less obvious and more subtle—and is likely to appear in any important conversation.

Prejudice will be recognized when another refuses to accept obvious facts or reasoned arguments yet has nothing to offer to the contrary. One cannot overcome prejudice by frontal assault. The folk saying goes, "A woman convinced against her will is of the same opinion still." The same applies to men. There is no point to winning an argument if it creates opposition. Said a businessman of a salesman who had just left his store, "He won the argument, but he lost the sale."

When personal prejudice is sensed as cause for failure to reach an agreement, one can try to shift the discussion away from the emotional basis. One can talk about the problem or about alternate solutions to the one which raises emotions. Many prejudiced people are unaware of their prejudice. Their preconceived ideas are based on their personal experiences or experiences of friends whom they trust. They find it hard to recognize that such experiences may be atypical or no longer applicable to changed circumstances in society.

For example, young people sometimes find older generations prejudiced. Since no respectable girl remained away from home after midnight in dad's youth, he cannot understand why his daughter should remain out until 1 a.m. for a graduation party.

People judge a group by one or two members of that group, i.e., corporation executives are heartless, union leaders are radicals, Yankees are penny-pinchers, southern women are scatter-brained. Such stereotyping is endless and based on single encounters and surface appearances.

Deeply-held prejudices are not likely to be changed in one conversation, but one can begin the process by asking questions which plant the seed of doubt. One can offer evidence to the contrary—experiences of one's own or of others whose view carries weight, statistics showing that the weight of evidence lies elsewhere, or suggestions about how people or situations are changing.

When encountering prejudice, it is imperative to permit the other person to save face and always leave an opening for a graceful change of mind. Doubt or disagreement must be offered gently to avoid confrontation. Sometimes a new experience will cause a person to completely reverse attitude.

A white woman with preconceived ideas about blacks was persuaded to join her Sunday School class in a special tutoring program for black youngsters. The purpose was to help them catch up with their age groups by overcoming handicaps caused by deficiencies of exposure in earlier childhood years. She agreed to help one talented black youngster and, in the process, became so fond of the boy that she altered her entire feelings about black people in general.

Listening as Communication

Thoughtful listening to why another does not agree enables one to adjust to the situation. Benjamin Franklin learned the value of advancing his own ideas hesitantly and tentatively. This not only enabled others to approach a matter more open-mindedly but also, he found, seemed to encourage them to look for strengths in his ideas rather than criticize—since he seemed unsure himself.

One who comes on strong appeals to our competitive instincts, and we rise to battle. Weakness appeals to our protective nature, and we feel a desire to help. Remembering this, we can appeal to the other person's better desires and acquire an ally rather than an enemy.

Sensitivity to other people's attitudes and moods is something we learn at an early age. One who is truly aware soon automatically senses when something is unacceptable and adjusts to the other person's reaction. One suppresses a desire to counter disagreement with stronger arguments or turn away completely and give up. One learns to ask, "Don't you agree?" and then to listen to the other's objections.

Opening a conversation, one must first establish contact with the other's interests and concerns. Media communicators know this—the pretty girl posed next to the new model car in an advertisement became a photographic cliche. Before speaking one's piece in a conversation, one needs to ensure the other is not too preoccupied with some problem of the moment to really listen to what one has to say.

Listening first and speaking later enables you to know on what level of need a person is operating. Dr. Abraham Maslow discovered people have five basic needs (in order of priority): physical, security, love, self-esteem, and self-actualization. Only people who are comfortable and feel secure are able to attend to their higher-level needs for group participation, achievement, recognition, and creative self-fulfillment. A man worried about a prospective operation or a woman concerned about a sick child is in no position to consider a leadership position in youth work. Nor will a man worried about the survival of his business be a likely prospect for the board of trustees.

On the other hand an able man passed over for a promotion but secure in his employment may well be a board candidate. He may find in the chairmanship of a United Way financial campaign just the outlet he needs for achievement and recognition. It may heal his bruised ego and serve to restore his sense of competence and self-esteem.

A woman who has raised her children, arranged her home the way she wants it and is secure in her husband's affection, will look for some new challenge. Homemakers with fewer responsibilities have long been the mainstay of charitable agencies, financial drives and political campaigns. So also are retired citizens with no more deadlines to meet good prospects for volunteer work.

By listening to what people talk about and what they say, you can learn to discover on what level they are operating, and how to appeal to them by nudging them in a direction they already want to go.

One other aspect of careful listening is feedback. People often "hear" what they want to hear or expect to hear. They can interpret what you have said completely opposite to what you intended, justifying this by a tone of voice which they interpret as ironical or an expression of disbelief in what you are saying. They may claim a suggestion of a wink of the eye is indication that you and they know that you must state certain things for the public or for the record, but that you both know differently.

It is always well when one has some doubt about whether an understanding has been reached to ask for the other to restate the matter in his own language. This feedback in a personal conversation has traditionally been followed by a handshake making the agreement binding on both parties in law in certain jurisdictions.

Communication With Professionals

Professionals are employed for their special knowledge and skills. This implies their advice will be sought about any proposal in their fields of expertise. They will expect to be treated as colleagues—to be consulted about programs in which they will participate both in the idea stage and before the programs are presented for final approval. Such staff members feel that they know the needs of the groups with which they are in touch (youths, working mothers, senior citizens, homemakers, and such) better than anyone else. Failure to consult them about how best to meet the needs of people whom they look upon as their clients is threatening to their own need for security and self-esteem.

The executive director is the key person in such internal communication, working toward a consensus which can prove viable and which he can conscientiously defend before the governing board. Some of the new generation of professionals create special problems for the director. Trained, knowledgeable and dedicated, they are often eager and impatient. They want to create overnight the perfect world they envision. Their demands are sometimes based on personal values, emotionally held. They may have no background of experience in dealing with unlimited demands and limited resources. They are prejudiced against anything traditional which they see as "establishment."

Under such circumstances, the executive may have difficulty in arriving at agreement on attainable proposals. Somehow he or she must bring the dissidents to realize that in an organization, no one can pursue his own individual way without consultation, that flexibility is needed for compromise. This is often easier in one-to-one conversations where a difficult matter is not viewed as a confrontation and where a dissident lacks a feeling of unity with others of the same outlook. Here concern for his or her personal need of the moment can be demonstrated without dilution by a need for equal attention to the others of a group.

In all such communication, however, if it appears that a relationship is not going to work, one might as well seek a way to terminate it and save one's energies for something which will. A situation may also arise of difficulty with older staff members unable to adjust to changing needs of the organization and its clientele.

Older staff members who have borne the burden of an organization through trying years have earned consideration and loyalty from even a new chief executive brought in to straighten an organization out. Yet he cannot permit their obstruction to stand in the way of serving new needs. The C.E. must realize that they need to be reassured against the threat to their feeling of professional security. In personal discussions, she or he must explore their needs to discover whether they can be involved in a new challenge, can be re-oriented through updating courses, or because of mental or physical deterioration need to be retired.

Some organizations provide retirement classes for persons reaching five years before retirement to help them with planning and mental preparation for this change of living. But, in the end, it will be the person-to-person listening and counseling which will resolve the situation.

Motivating Volunteers

Every personal relationship has an aspect of mutuality. Each gives something to it; each gets something from it. If this assumed exchange is not satisfactory to either party, he or she can break it. Best relations are those in which two work together for shared objectives.

In the case of staff members there is the additional matter of salary for which they relinquish their own preferences on many work matters to the direction of the organization as a whole. Volunteers may be assumed to have selfless dedication to the organization's objectives in most cases. There are, however, other incentives which motivate people to service without compensation.

In enlisting and choosing volunteer leaders, it is especially important to learn their personal motivation and whether this motivation has staying power. One needs to discover the volunteer's self-image and to lead him or her in a direction in which he or she would normally go. It can be disastrous to enlist a volunteer for a task which violates the self-image.

When friends mistakenly persuade someone to undertake some task because of the organization's need and not because the person feels qualified, it can lead to a desire to resign. Don't ask a man who likes to work behind the scenes to head a financial campaign. Some people don't enjoy being out front.

A man who was a back-slapper, dropped names, had held prominent offices in his church, was nevertheless not a leader. He would ask of his every proposal, "Does this seem sound?" Over quiet protests about his lack of ability for the job, he was made chairperson of an important community organization. It turned out that he was not just being modest. He was a failure. He had been happy just being "one of the boys."

This instance emphasizes the importance of the responsibility of those who pull strings behind the scenes to those whose lives they affect. Once a man or woman has accepted a volunteer leadership role, the executive and staff owe him or her full support in what he or she has undertaken. The C.E. must know the person's strengths and weaknesses, provide that the situations with which he or she must cope are not self-destroying but ones encouraging growth and development.

Prime potential leaders are those who have supported reasonable proposals, have shown good judgment of people and their motivations, are dedicated and purposeful, are willing to listen extensively to others, can assert themselves when the situation calls for action.

A chief executive has certain goals for the organization and the chairman, let us say, has certain personal goals. There is a case of ethics here. Some chairpersons love the spotlight and wish to enlarge their personal image with the public regardless of the organization's priorities. Everyone has conflicting emotions and desires. The C.E. in his personal conversations must help the chairperson to resolve his/her inner conflicts and overcome the hangups which prevent him/her from succeeding in the task undertaken.

Once volunteer leaders have accepted prominent assignments, they also need constant reassurance of the wisdom of their decision, competent supportive staff work, and sympathetic guidance. Sometimes, a person with vexing problems at home or at work may be led to immerse himself or herself in the larger concerns of the organization and find relief from inner tensions which have been building up.

Dealing With Criticism

"Some of my biggest contributors and best supporters on the board of directors resulted from criticism," says a former director of a social service agency. New at the job, he was buttonholed one day by a ten-year member who criticized a new policy of scheduling events for youngsters and senior citizens in the building at the same hours.

The new director explained the policy was deliberate. Young people and adults need exposure to each other, he explained. If the youngsters running noisily about the hallways was unacceptable, it was the fault of management for failing to train them in acceptable behavior.

The older member persisted that the agency needed a much stronger health program for the adults who were being neglected. The director at once agreed with him, saying, "I'd like to talk to you further about that." He made an appointment with him and came to the interview with notes he had made about a program he would like to see implemented.

"I want you to understand this is not at present an objective of the association, nor do I presently recommend it to them," he said, "but I would like to share it with you and get your ideas." The member was not only interested, but made constructive suggestions which the director at once incorporated into his plan.

The chief roadblock to the plan, the director pointed out, was lack of parking space in the vicinity. Executives could not carry on constructive physical exercise programs if they had to interrupt them to go outside and place more coins in street parking meters. He expressed hope that a next door neighbor's plan to move from the vicinity would make it possible to purchase an adjoining lot and create a parking area.

"Find out how much it will cost," said the member in parting.

The director did, and he received from the member a check to cover the cost of land purchase.

Personal communication with an important leader or contributor does not necessarily call for agreement with his or her point of view. It does require dialogue—with honesty and receptivity. It means resistance to a tendency to argue when criticism seems like an attack against you or what you are doing. It means listening thoughtfully to criticism to see whether it has merit.

If it is based on misinformation, provide the facts. If it is given with goodwill, offer to think about it—and do. If, as so often happens, a critic provides you with a whole new way of looking at a matter, be sure to tell him/her so at the earliest opportunity. There are few, if any, better ways to turn critics into solid supporters. It gives the other the satisfaction of having made a genuine contribution.

Avoid Conversation Stoppers

One problem in conversational communication is the use of trigger words or flat statements which "turn people off." Consider this conversation stopper:

A man approaches the town's wealthiest citizen to ask for a contribution toward the construction of an outdoor swimming pool. His approach goes something like this:

"Don't you think the children of this community need a place to swim during the summer school vacation?"

The man replies, "I hate noisy kids!"

The solicitor has tried to follow the rule of posing the problem before asking support for a solution. But he has failed to consider fully the prospect's point of view. He quickly recovers and starts over where he should have started the first time.

"It has been suggested that we need to do something to get the youngsters off the streets and keep them out of mischief during school vacations. What do you think?"

Without committing himself, the solicitor has related someone else's suggestion. He is free to go along strategically with the prospect's reactions and the latter is free to consider the problem with an open mind.

Whatever his response now, it is unlikely to be a conversation stopper. The solicitor can continue to offer new evidence for his consideration. Presenting a problem invites reason and sympathetic response. By contrast, an invitation to support a solution before the other has had a chance to consider a matter thoroughly is to risk a conversation stopper.

An agency director who believes guidelines are needed to keep conversation flowing has trained his entire staff to listen for what people really mean instead of accepting their words at face value.

A mother calls to ask about the qualifications of an aquatics director. He responds, "What you really want to know is whether he can help your child. Right?" Then he reviews how this man has been trained to take a personal interest in each child's development, not just to concentrate on those "with Olympic potential." He cites his director's record of performance with "average" youngsters as well as those with championship qualities.

A stranger calls to ask what a membership costs. The telephone operator is trained to avoid such a conversation stopper as, "The fee is $100," by quickly adding, "Let me turn you over to the program director who can explain all the services that covers."

The program director then picks up this cue by probing for any reason for hesitation because of cost. Is the caller concerned about being able to pay the annual fee all at once? Perhaps an installment plan can be worked out. Does she perhaps come within the group which need and will qualify for scholarship assistance?

Flat statements are often conversation stoppers because they indicate a closed mind. Instead of disagreeing, the other person may turn away without a word, avoiding what would appear to be a confrontation. Trigger words are ones that arouse emotions. Often perfectly good words take on overtones never intended. **Discrimination** and **busing** were positive, useful words until they became associated with racial strife. Now they may be conversation stoppers for persons who are tired of endless arguments about them in today's context.

As long as there is an opportunity to make a person-to-person conversation fruitful, it is desirable to keep the discussion going. But, even when ending a fruitless discussion, avoid conversation stoppers so that consideration of the problem can later be resumed in a more favorable atmosphere.

CHAPTER VII

MAKING TELEPHONING PRODUCTIVE

As a communication medium, telephoning is taken too much for granted. Familiar with the instrument from childhood, most present-day citizens pick up the receiver and dial without hesitation. To some professionals, realizing how much time they spend daily at making and receiving calls comes as a shock.

This is especially true of some public relations professionals who have been trained and experienced in the newspaper or other print media. From their work backgrounds, they have become visually minded and overlook the importance of verbal communication.

Convenience and time-saving are great telephone assets. The agency head who said, "Unless I spend one-third of my time on the telephone, I'm not doing my job," added: "Conflicting schedules make assembling committees difficult, so I talk to people by phone—day or night. When they're available, I'm available."

With trustees, large contributors and key leadership, this necessity is obvious. What may not be equally obvious is the telephone's importance in communicating with members, prospects and clients. The public's impression of some organizations is built largely on how well its people handle their phone calls.

Very often one's first personal contact with an agency is a phone call, perhaps inquiring about some program about which one has read in a newspaper or in response to a direct mail promotion. A person who finds this first experience frustrating or unpleasant may never get in touch again.

Perhaps a call may be from a prospective donor whose enthusiasm has been sparked by some creative project and who wants to know more about it from the program director before deciding to support it. Or, it may be from someone who needs the agency's help. Whatever the reason, the caller is entitled to a courteous hearing and to be placed in touch with someone who can respond.

Provide Enough Telephones

First step in making certain people can communicate with your agency by phone is to have enough phone lines. On one occasion, the author called a hospital repeatedly over a period of two hours, getting nothing but busy signals. This might have been excusable during an emergency or an epidemic. But when this happens under normal circumstances, the circuits are inadequate. For a caller to persist over a period of time means that the purpose of his or her telephoning must be important and pressing.

One executive who received complaints on this score turned to his local phone company and was pleased to learn that it could provide a telephone survey. This included monitoring the numbers of incoming and outgoing calls for each department and unit so that management could judge where and how many phones were needed. The monitoring also included calls which did not get through.

More phones require more people to answer them—but not always. Consider these situations:

Make Certain Phones Are Covered

One man called a medical office and let the phone ring fifty times before hanging up in disgust. Under such circumstances a caller envisions that everyone is out for a coffee break. This may not be fair. A harried telephone-receptionist may have three phones ringing at once. Or, a waiting patient may have suffered a heart attack, and the operator is summoning help. Whatever the cause, there are ways of preventing non-coverage.

Normally, a caller should expect an answer before the phone has rung more than five times; but under no circumstances would he or she expect to wait more than ten rings when calling an organization during regular office hours.

Agencies can remedy the overload situation by having a person otherwise assigned available to take over excess incoming calls at peak periods or on signal from the operator in an emergency. Smaller agencies may wish to consider an answering service or an automatic answering device as a less expensive substitute or supplement.

Consider An Answering Service or Device

Agencies whose clients may need to call them in off-hours when the offices are closed may find an answering device or answering service worth while. Either a service's operators or a recorded message on a device can instruct callers how to reach someone to help them in an emergency.

Answering services may be more expensive, but have distinct advantages. While a recorder device can give out another number to be called, a service operator can take down a caller's number and try to reach a staff member or executive. Some persons feel frustrated when getting a recorded message with no assurance of when they can receive a return call. Just to know that a live operator is aware of their problems and is trying to do something about them helps.

Once a board member of an organization flying back from an out-of-town meeting changed her travel plans when the weather turned bad and her plane flight was cancelled. Without sufficient change for a long distance charge, she had only a few minutes to notify a staff member who was to meet her at the airport. It was after five o'clock and the office was closed, but the answering service accepted the collect call and reached the staff member at home in time to save a half hour's drive. The staff member picked her up at the bus station in time to make a late speaking engagement.

When a recording device is used for telephone answering, messages to callers should be brief. They should give the name and, for the wrong-number callers, the phone number of the agency. Also, the name of the person speaking makes it more personal. Advise when someone will be available to return the call. Ask for the caller's name, phone number and reason for calling. Tell the caller the time limit for recording the message, and urge him/her if message is longer than the time allowed to call again and complete it.

Improve Staff's Telephone Techniques

Telephone training, often available from the telephone company, can accomplish wonders for an institution's relations with its public. Telephone operators and secretaries are logical candidates for this training. But executives and administrators who have never attended a seminar in telephoning may also improve from this exposure.

Here are a few basics in courtesies and techniques which everyone should know:

- Talk in a normal voice with mouth an inch away from the mouthpiece. Nearer may make words sound muffled—farther away may make them sound weak. Shouting to be heard may actually be painful to someone with the receiver close to his ear. Speak distinctly and at a moderate speed so that words do not sound jumbled.

- If a connection is poor or there is noise on the circuit, both parties should hang up. (On long distance calls particularly, attempting to communicate by repeating or shouting leads to extra time charges and possibilities of misunderstanding.) The original caller should then dial his or her operator, explain the situation, and ask for a good connection.

- Business calls should be as brief as practical. By courtesy, the calling party says goodby first. This is courteous. But when callers are long-winded, the one called may have to close the conversation tactfully.

- Any person answering a telephone should identify the organization reached and the person answering when it is not an operator. Some prefer to answer by giving the number only. For image building this has disadvantages. Numbers may be heard, as well as dialed, wrongly; it make take several moments in this case to straighten matters out. Moreover, people need to envision to whom they are talking for best communication.

- Speak in a friendly, interested voice. Do not try to do other work while carrying on a phone conversation. Even routine work, like signing letters, may make one sound distracted and preoccupied.

- Keep phone conversations to the point. Tying up an office phone with personal business or a sports event discussion may prevent important business from getting through.

Where these matters become a problem, a good-natured set of guide rules posted on the bulletin board or circulated among staff may help. Also, your telephone company may offer instructional sessions for your personnel or provide booklets on telephone effectiveness.

Management Action for Phoning Efficiency

Agencies can contribute in a number of ways to efficient phone use. One can make certain the operator, or whoever else receives incoming calls, is thoroughly briefed and continually kept informed on all matters likely to be the subjects of phone inquiries. The operator should know the names of all personnel or have handy a complete guide indicating departmental and individual extensions, so he or she can route calls without delay. Another essential is a calendar of events for answering inquiries about hours and places of meetings and courses. This avoids a need to refer callers to others for simple answers, perhaps causing them to wait and tying up a line.

Preparations must be made to handle extra phone traffic which can be anticipated. When publicity, program promotion or some special drive is likely the cause of a switchboard traffic jam, the operator should be briefed. Departments handling such promotions may need to enlist the help of others and instruct them in advance. The operator will then need to know of the alternate extensions to which he or she can refer such calls. The goal is to handle calls politely and efficiently and quickly clear the lines for other calls.

Where available, phone company training courses may be best. In their absence, management can improve performance through such guidelines as these:

• Before putting a call on hold, an operator should let a caller state his or her business. Few things are more frustrating than to dial for some time getting busy signals, then finally to reach an operator who says, "Just a moment, please," and without waiting for an explanation, lets the line go dead for five minutes. This is particularly annoying when you call long distance and are paying for waiting time.

• If an operator must ask a caller to wait, she or he should leave the decision up to the caller. Say, "That extension is busy. Will you wait?" If the answer is, "Yes," the operator should check back every two minutes during the delay with an explanation that the line is still busy. Thus the caller does not feel forgotten. If the decision at any point is to wait no longer, give the caller the option of leaving name and number for a call back.

· Specialists recommend no operator handle more than four lines. This might vary somewhat with the style of switchboard, kind of agency, and nature of the traffic. An increasingly popular dial-through system eliminates many switchboard problems for those who call, or are called, frequently and where individual executive or staff members' numbers are therefore known.

· Avoid cliches and stereotyped opening greetings, such as "Hello." Give agency name promptly. In more relaxed situations, a cheerful "Good morning, XYZ Agency" may be appropriate. An operator with a good voice and personality can do much toward creating an image for the organization.

· Secretaries should avoid such excuses as, "The director is in conference." He or she may very well be, but this has been abused too much by over-zealous secretaries to "protect" their bosses and by others at bosses' direction when, for some reason, they have not wanted to talk to a calling party. After a while this excuse leads to a conclusion that the boss has little time for anything but conferences. "Out" or "on a coffee break" are in bad taste. Better than an excuse which may not be true or acceptable, say, "Mrs. Jones is not available just now. May someone else help you?"

A specific reason recognized by the caller as having priority is most acceptable: "Mrs. Jones is on duty at our annual meeting and won't be available until next week. Meanwhile, can I be of help?"

· Operators of busy switchboards must be adept at determining the nature of calls quickly, giving a prompt answer or passing the call along to someone else. All this without seeming abrupt, rude or indifferent. The image of an agency must be one of people who care. At all times the operator must maintain an attitude of friendly helpfulness without letting her efficiency show through.

· Recording of phone messages requires system. A phone

answerer will do better if provided with a slip (mimeographed or printed) with spaces for caller's name, affiliation, phone number, hour called, message, instructions whether to return the call, and the urgency. Space for each item prevents overlooking some vital point. Wording which permits checking off or circling rather than writing out details cuts time, increases efficiency: Will Call Again____; Please Return call____. Call between hours: ____ to ____ A.M., P.M. Will write details ____.

By instruction, person taking a call should put the message slip in some agreed upon place where it will be visible and not be covered up by incoming mail. Secretaries should call the executive's attention to important and pressing ones at once on her/his return.

• When necessary to transfer a call to another department, one must take care to explain the circumstances to the caller. Otherwise, the caller may become confused, believing he or she is speaking with the same person, and fail to repeat essential information for the new recipient.

• When a staff member takes a call which he or she cannot handle satisfactorily, it is often better to suggest that the caller leave his number for a call-back. Locating the right person may take some time. In a large, well-known organization, a caller has been known to be shifted to four different persons before finding someone who could help. All this because an operator originally misinterpreted a caller's specific interest.

Face to face, we interpret facial expression to judge a person's mood and attitude. On the phone, the voice provides clues to the same. Whether face to face or phoning, expression and voice tone generally match. A business firm placed mirrors in front of its operators to remind them of the impression they were giving to others. It worked.

How to Make a Successful Telephone Call

Business phoning requires a different approach from the casualness of social conversation. Whether one should be formal or informal will depend on the relative status of the two parties and how well they know each other. Natural personalities will and should come through. But even with friends, it should not be forgotten that the call is purposeful—both parties are presumably using up time for which their organizations are paying. It is not appropriate to discuss last night's football—unless, for example, you are a salesman and the other party is a prospect or you need something for a warm-up and know the other is a fan.

Here are a few guidelines for making a phone call successful:

• Plan the call in advance. Write down points to be covered in the order you want to take them up. Check each off as completed. Make certain in advance you have any needed facts in front of you and files to which you may need to refer at hand. Review the conversation as you anticipate it will go and make certain in your own mind that telephoning is the best method for communicating. (E.g.: Is this so important you should see the other person, or would a letter do? In some instances, you may want to send a letter before phoning, so that you both have the same information in front of you.)

• If you know the person, envision the face as you dial. This helps overcome in your mind the handicap of not being able to see the facial expression.

• Listen to the tone of voice and match the other's mood. If you sense hesitation, inquire whether you are interrupting something and when would it be convenient for you to call again. You cannot see the other's situation. Perhaps there are too many pressing things for him/her to give you full attention just then.

• Address the other by name and identify yourself promptly. Don't expect the person called to recognize your voice even if you are friends. Say, "Mr. Jones, this is Albert Ruskin of the Urban Center in Smithtown."

• Make certain you have the right person. If there is any doubt don't hesitate to ask, "Is this Edward Jones in the camping equipment department?" Nothing can be more embarrassing than for a client to launch a long recitation of a personal problem only to find that, in a switchboard mixup, the call has been confused with another one for a social service worker.

• Listen closely for clues to the other's reaction. Another

voice in the background may indicate an unanticipated interruption at the other end of the line. You may no longer be receiving the other's full attention.

• Plan to call at convenient times. If you do not know the other's habits, it is often wise to avoid the first hour of the morning for long calls. This time is often devoted to arranging the day or reading mail. On the other hand, for some executives this is the best time before they become involved in long staff meetings which are difficult to interrupt.

Also good to avoid is the last hour of the afternoon when the person called may be mentally exhausted from an ambitious schedule or rushing to complete an end-of-the-day cleanup.

• Jot down notes on the conversation—either as you talk, or immediately after the conversation is completed. Note particularly any matters to be followed up and who is to be responsible, also any agreements which are to be confirmed in writing.

• Sometimes it is appropriate to review points covered with the other before signing off the conversation with a "thank you" and "goodby."

Keeping Telephone Costs in Line

In organizations with more than a handful of staff people, telephone costs at times seem to expand out of control. Guidelines for making telephone usage more productive and less costly include:

• Discourage personal calls on organization phones during business hours unless absolutely necessary.

• Encourage personnel to make all calls brief and to the point. Some agencies supply their people with minute sand timers. It is astonishing how valuable a minimum one-minute long distance call can be when the only answer you seek is a prompt "yes" or "no."

• Call suppliers collect. Sometimes they will refuse a call but call you back on their toll-free WATS lines. In calling a government agency, you can ask the operator you reach to contact the person you want and ask him or her to call you back.

• Use free WX or 800 toll numbers. Many companies now

have these for the convenience of far-flung customers. There is a modestly-priced directory of such numbers or you can get the information from "800 Information Operator."

- Call across time zones in the cheaper off-hours.

- Use person-to-person calling when your party may not be immediately available. Time rates are higher but charges do not start until your party is on the line.

- Dial direct.

- Keep a list of frequently called numbers for time-saving reference. Phone companies supply phone list books.

- Call by appointment. Arrangements can be made by letter or by use of the one-minute special rate.

- Use conference calls to save travel time and costs when three or more people must be involved in a discussion.

- When going out, leave word when you will return. Don't leave your phone uncovered. If no one else can answer it, have operator take messages and hold for your return. Advise how you can be reached in an emergency, and when you expect to return—save charges for having to call the other and apologize.

When to Telephone

The telephone is a versatile communication medium. Use the telephone when. . .

- Personal touch is valuable and face-to-face communication is impractical.

- When immediacy is important.

- When a written record is unnecessary or can be supplied afterward for confirmation.

- When the stenographic pool is overloaded.

- When the other party already has background information and a phone appeal can push for a decision.

- To keep in touch with the leadership group and other high priority communication.

- To save travel time and expense.

* To get through and make an impression when other communication fails. Some people will accept a phone call who won't answer a letter.

* To back up an appeal by mail.

Phone Hints for Executives

Keep a telephone log. This is a daily record of phone calls completed, subject matter covered, agreements reached. This is a planning tool for those who manage-by-objective to enable them to check whether they have covered the ground as anticipated and whether any group of constituents have been overlooked and neglected. It can also serve to settle disputes or misunderstandings when memories disagree.

Check your agency's telephone image. Call your office from time to time, disguising your voice, or monitor someone else's call to see how your staff handles phone inquiries. Does it check with the image you want your organization to project and with the instructions and guidelines you have issued?

CHAPTER VIII

STAFF MEETINGS AS COMMUNICATION MEDIUM

Properly conducted staff meetings can accomplish several important communication objectives:

- Define agency policies in terms of working objectives.
- Translate these objectives into short-term goals.
- Assign responsibility for goals among staff members.
- Develop strategies to carry out programs for achieving goals.
- Evaluate each goal in terms of its contribution to overall objectives.
- Set time frames for accomplishment of tasks.
- Develop in staff members a sense of appreciation for the abilities and skills of each other.
- Make staff members aware of organizational problems and involve them in solutions.
- Provide each member with an understanding of the program as a whole and create staff loyalties to overall objectives.
- Monitor progress and feedback.

In staff meetings, unity of attitudes and purposes can be developed to make a group of individuals into an organization. In larger organizations especially, there can develop a tendency to become divided and departmentalized. Staff people work with problems in their own assigned areas until, to them, these become the most important work of the organization. Sometimes they seem to feel that their department's importance is greater than the rest of the organization.

Of course, everyone should feel a pride in his or her own work. But, it is even more essential that in all conversations each should be able to explain and "sell" the agency's program in its entirety. Both inside and outside an organization, every employee is a communicator. What she or he says about it will contribute to its public image and to its success in meeting its objectives.

When the Objective is Planning

Every staff meeting should have a purpose, or purposes, in the mind of the chief executive before it is called. The nature of the meeting and the way it is conducted will be determined by that purpose. One important type is the planning session.

One agency executive holds a two-day meeting of all staff members before the year's activities get under way. At this gathering programs are developed in broad outlines and assigned tentative priorities. Later they are presented to an expanded board—all trustees plus key supervisors—which reviews and approves them.

These two meetings include and involve all persons who are vitally important to the year's successful operations. Once they have offered their ideas and agreed upon what should be done, all have an interest in making the program succeed whether by contributing the necessary finances or carrying out the day-by-day implementation.

Even with planning sessions, the executive needs to have objectives specifically in mind in order to conserve staff time. In a two-day series of meetings, an objective for each session will be advisable: Determine New Course Subjects for Hi-Y Leadership Development; Establish Guidelines for Re-Locating Summer Camp; etc. The presiding officer can help by announcing the objective at the beginning of the session and showing how it relates to a goal set by the governing board. This then becomes a framework for keeping the discussions pointed toward the objective.

Where everyone comes to a subject of a discussion without previous experience or plan to offer, the chairperson may decide to hold a brain-storming session. In this case the ground rules are free and easy. Everyone is asked to give his or her ideas as they come to mind without examining their worth. Some person is named clerk to take them all down. The point is that one idea, even a foolish one, stimulates other ideas. Out of this, may come a few suggestions worth considering. Someone will later evaluate them. Such sessions, when everyone understands that they are not to be held accountable for ideas nor credited with them, free creative minds to roam at will. At times these produce solutions which would have been hard to reach in any other way.

At other sessions, program directors may come with well-formed plans based on previous years' experience. In such instances, the session's objective may be to review the plan for any oversights or criticisms. Or a plan may sometimes be so well formulated that the program is presented largely as a matter of information for other departments and to make certain of cooperation and support of all non-participants.

In such cases, those in attendance are entitled to advance notice so that they are not embarrassed at making comments out of order.

In most planning conferences, the "big picture" is reviewed first—policy decisions, overall objectives, the image the organization is seeking to create. Those who are old-timers may feel they know these things, but new members need this. No staffer is in position to speak to the question or evaluate others' suggestions without this briefing.

Executives conducting planning sessions must be prepared to avoid showing astonishment at the insights some new staffers may offer. The moderator must determine whether or not the suggestions are in conflict with the program as a whole, or just with details. Are those making the suggestions totally unsuited to the organization because their own objectives are in conflict? Or perhaps are these the most perceptive and capable people— ahead of the rest in their thinking?

Sometimes the persons who seem to be nit-pickers are the ones who care most about the project under discussion. Once sold, they may turn out to be the most enthusiastic supporters of the program.

Often planning sessions will be more productive if the attendees are provided with outlines and background material for study in advance so that they can frame their comments before they get on their feet.

Brief Meetings With One Purpose

Another type of meeting is the single purpose meeting. Such staff meetings are more apt to be held during the busy part of the year when staff members are involved in carrying out their program responsibilities. Since less time is available at that season, meetings are kept brief unless a subject demands long discussion.

This type of meeting may be for information only with only questions for better understanding invited. Or if the executive wants different points of view he can ask that they be summarized and details submitted later in writing. The point here is to discover whether there is a consensus, or failing that, what divergencies in points of view exist.

Executive Makes Staff Meetings Efficient

Staff meetings can be lengthy, perhaps need to be in the planning stage. But one executive decided some of his program directors had developed a taste for discussion as a means of avoiding decisions and action after the time for action arrived.

His remedy was drastic. He set regular times for meetings, limited them to one hour each. He announced the objective of each meeting well in advance so each staffer might arrive prepared to streamline his remarks. He called for sharpened reasoning and crisp conclusions. It worked.

Progress reports were kept to the facts, projections to specifics. Persons who rambled off the subject were promptly called to order.

This drastic action, applied only during the peak seasons, illustrates one point: Staff meetings are a costly method of communication unless the executive plans them, controls them, and makes certain they are productive.

Another executive often talks over in advance with key department heads what he hopes will come out of a meeting. Thus they can support his objectives and move the discussions along.

On occasion, a ten minute staff meeting may be quite sufficient. When all the ideas have been contributed and planning is completed, when each person has had an opportunity to have questions answered and has received any work materials needed, the only things left may be to announce final decisions and exhort everyone to "get going" on assignments.

Depending on size and centralized location of an organization, some agencies on occasion assemble their entire staff, not just professionals and department heads. Customarily, a manager can rely on printed bulletins and department heads to pass along whatever information service employees need and want to know. But at times some of these may be overheard to remark, "I don't understand why we are doing this," or, "I don't know what I am supposed to do." These comments indicate a breakdown in communications and an investigation of the specific case—or perhaps a general staff briefing—may be indicated.

For morale's sake it may also be desirable on occasion to announce some new major project at a general staff meeting so that all can share enthusiasm and sense the importance of their own efforts in making it succeed. Program architects who have lived with the new enterprise through its birthing may feel they have heard enough of it by then and that their presence is unnecessary. Yet their attendance will enhance its importance in the eyes of their co-workers and service employees. And mention of their part in it will advance their status among the rest of the employees.

Conferences for Monitoring and Feedback

Staff meetings may be called by the executive to find out what is happening in an organization. One C.E. has found this is his best way of keeping up with all the developments in a diversified institution. He calls on each person responsible for a department or program to report on activities and progress.

This type of meeting has additional values. By letting the other professionals see what each is doing, they may learn from the more experienced and capable associates and be spurred to greater efforts toward the goals in their own fields of responsibility.

This C.E., at the beginning of each staff conference, announces his agenda for the session. He asks his associates whether they have additional items they would like to have discussed, and adds these to the list. He also considers suggestions for alterations in the agenda. A department head may have run into a problem he/she would rather discuss privately than in open meeting. Or, he/she may not wish to report progress prematurely.

This C.E.'s staff meetings are directed, but not shut off.

"You must give staff members a chance to establish a pecking order," he says. He usually sets priorities because of timing, but allows his associates to satisfy their egos. He speaks last, and only when he has something to say. He tries to draw as many into a discussion as possible. He believes that each must make a contribution so that each feels he or she is a participant in the decision.

In order to give importance to every staff member, the C.E. makes notes of what each woman or man has said. He picks up apt phrases they have used. At the end of each conference he summarizes the discussion from his own point of view. He uses the phrases of others, incorporates their ideas with credit to the person offering it. While the final product, as he reviews it, may not meet the criteria or requirements a specific individual has advocated, nevertheless all persons can see how their own thinking has helped to advance the thinking of all.

This C.E. finds that in this way he best gets to know how well management objectives are being implemented, and how clients and others in the community are responding to agency programs. He also gets a sense of staff members as individuals, how they differ from each other, their strengths and their weaknesses. By questioning, he can diplomatically call on each to justify his or her program activities in terms of clients' needs and organization goals, and any assignment of resources in relation to requirements of other agency units.

This same executive likes to use staff conferences to generate job assignments. Working with the professional group to determine the necessary tasks to reach goals, he finds all see what needs to be done and then together divide up the job segments among themselves. This democratic method saves him from having to make such decisions and from individual resentment over what someone might otherwise consider arbitrary decisions.

His philosophy is:

"An autocrat says, 'Do it my way.' But he can't always make people accept this. Under such a system, busyness becomes a virtue as each tries to appear to be justifying himself. Attending meetings is not an objective in itself; it can become make-work. I have found you can get a lot more done if you leave the **how** to the professionals who are doing the job."

Staff Meetings for Problem Solving

Tough problems sometimes require the best ideas of all staff people for their solution. This is particularly true when all must be involved in the solutions. When one staff member neglects his or her responsibilities or departs from established goals and guidelines, it may be easier to correct by a staff approach.

In one central city agency the director had difficulty communicating with his young professional staff. For one thing, he found, they were ill-equipped with mastery of words, grammar and syntax to write without great effort. After a staff member had labored at the typewriter to produce a memorandum, or struggled to design and post a sign, he would consider he had performed a day's work and filled his responsibility.

A case in point was that of a young member of the athletics staff who had prepared and circulated the rules and posted a sign against boys walking on the basketball court with street shoes rather than sneakers. He would constantly walk by youngsters violating the rule without even calling the matter to their attention.

The solution was a staff meeting at which was discussed the damage to the court from such practices, a review of the costs of re-waxing and consequent drain of resources which might otherwise be available for other projects. In this light, fellow staff members put pressure on the one avoiding responsibility to enforce the rules.

Some executives use brain-storming sessions for solving problems even where these are not of broad staff concern. Too often those who have long struggled with a matter are too close to look at it with perspective. This method has long worked successfully in a scientific staff. In one instance, a chemist asked for help on how to handle a problem with chicle, the sticky base for chewing gum. A metallurgist observed, "If that were our problem, we would freeze it, then grind it into powder which makes it easy to handle."

In colleges, interdisciplinary studies have forced academic people to cross previous lines of demarcation to help each other in the interest of the objective: helping the student. This has shown that staff meetings can—through cross-over of insights—become valuable problem-solvers in human affairs as well as science.

Calling Staff Conferences

Should an executive call staff meetings for first thing in the morning? Some C.E.'s have—where tardiness has become a real problem, or in order to get minds together, while they are still free from involvement in the day's problems. For administrators this can pose a problem if they are accustomed to using the first hour for assigning the day's tasks to subordinates or handling the morning mail.

Whenever staff meetings are held they are bound to be inconvenient for someone. Best insurance against this is to give plenty of notice; if an emergency meeting must be called, make it brief, and say so at the start. What you want is the best attention people can give, not half-hearted attention while worried about whether some project is going forward as planned though unsupervised.

Luncheon meetings have their advantages if discussions are non-worrisome, but stressful matters are not conducive to digestion and health. After lunch, meetings are likely to find some staffers still drowsy. Late afternoon meetings prevent handling telephone callbacks and signing mail. For communication, no one ideal time exists. C.E.'s will select a time which experience shows best suits the flow of work in their own organization.

Another decision is whether to invite a full staff or only selected people who would be concerned with a project. The C.E. who first establishes his objective for a meeting and analyzes the nature of problems to be discussed can best decide whether the expense in time of those not directly concerned will be worthwhile. In case these latter are asked to attend, they should be informed of the reason. Otherwise some non-involved staffer may be wondering, "Why am I sitting here when I could be making certain the dues statements are mailed on time?"

Concluding a staff meeting may be as important as the discussion itself. The C.E., as presiding officer, can summarize the discussion, unifying the impressions of those present, sharpening the points of those which were hazily made, evaluating whether the objective was reached, noting who is to take what actions as a result. If the executive does not himself keep the notes of the meeting, he may want to assign someone else the task of summarizing what has taken place and circulating a meeting report to all present.

CHAPTER IX

THE SPOKEN MESSAGE

Organizations may use speakers as a medium of communication in two ways:

. Spokespersons who present the institution's point of view and programs to meetings of outside groups, prospects, members, clients, and the general public.

. Outside speakers who bring knowledge and other points of view to an agency's staff or other persons involved in the agency's staff.

Reasons for inviting a speaker from outside vary widely. One might be a desire to "shake up" an organization which is in a rut by exposing its staff or members to the work or views of others with similar objectives. Or one might find that someone who has been notably successful in a project could provide skills and insights not available within one's own agency.

One agency head who could not seem to get a point across to his own people himself decided that a friend who headed another agency and was a stranger to them might communicate his message more successfully. In this case, it worked.

Sometimes an institution wants to offer an important person a platform—for the publicity value or because the leaders wish to interest that person in their own work. This might be a foundation head, a wealthy philanthropist or business man, or someone in an important media position. An organization dependent in part on state financial support might well consider inviting the governor or a state senator of influence in the appropriations process.

In these cases, the purpose is essentially to make a personal contact in a favorable environment. While the speaker is communicating to you on one of his or her favorite topics, your people have an opportunity to ask questions, to relate it to your organization's work. On your home ground, you also have an opportunity to show your agency in operation—more effective than any verbal description.

When You Invite Someone to Speak

Let's suppose that you have decided to invite a "name speaker" for an annual benefit dinner-dance. Whether or not the person is a good speaker, you are certain the announcement of the name will attract a large crowd. Here are a few guidelines others have found helpful.

. Invite the speaker well in advance. Popular speakers are sometimes booked for a year ahead. Most busy people have well-filled schedules and need to block out the time for preparation and delivery. Early reservation is also an advantage when you have selected a date which is popular and need time to find a substitute.

• When making plans, consider why you are inviting the speaker and make out a list of several possibilities who fit your requirements. Assign a priority to each and start with your first choice.

• Be explicit in your invitation as to what, if any honorarium you offer and whether you will pay travel and other expenses. It can be embarrassing to you if this has not been settled in advance and you are uncertain of details when the speaker raises the question.

• Be specific about the size and nature of the audience he or she will address, the time allotted for the speech, details of what will proceed and follow the speaker, any unusual or characteristic aspects of the occasion which will give a picture of the situation he or she will face.

This information may also help persuade your speaker to accept. Prominent people who have refused to travel a few blocks for a substantial fee to address some large audience have been known to travel across the country at their own expense to speak to a small audience—of people who interest them and on the right occasion.

- If invitation is first extended by telephone, confirm it at once in writing with all details mentioned unless the invitation is rejected out of hand. Many will want time to consider what is involved before giving a final "Yes."

- Confirm receipt of an acceptance at once in writing, expressing your pleasure. If out-of-town speaker, inform him/her of local arrangements—hotel accommodations, reception before or after the occasion with indication of invitees, best methods of transportation. Offer to meet plane or train.

- Reserve hotel room if part of the arrangement and make certain bill will come to you, so speaker will have no embarrassment in checking out.

- Send speaker list of your officers, head table diners, or other people of prominence he/she may meet. If others will also speak, give their names and topics. Provide background of reason for the occasion and any local references he/she might want to use in the address.

- Send speaker a reminder letter ten days before the speaking date with any last minute details—or telephone.

- Meet plane or train early. Traffic jams or other foul ups can cause delay and embarrassment. The task of arrangements is not complete until the speaker is introduced to the presiding officer and any other people of importance on the program.

- Prepare an introduction which is appropriate to the occasion and gives a minimum of details, but highlight some incident about the guest which illustrates the personality of his/her connection with the evening's topic. A secretary or friend may be able to help in advance with this.

- Keep the introduction short. Remember it is the speaker people came to hear.

- Escort the speaker to hotel, airport or station, as case may be, afterward. Take this opportunity to express your thanks for coming.

- If the speaker comes without charge, a token gift is appropriate—on leaving or mailed later.

- Send a letter of appreciation on behalf of your group, preferably signed by your chairperson or other appropriate official. On occasion, a resolution of appreciation or certificate on authority of the governing board may be desirable.

- Mail the speaker clippings of any accounts of his address in the press or copies of the publications in which it appeared.

When You Are Asked to Speak

Almost anyone who can talk effectively person-to-person should be able to learn to address an audience. A great obstacle for many people seems to be self-consciousness when they stand in the spotlight and realize that they are expected to do all the talking. But, most people, even those who have spoken many times to large audiences, have a mild case of jitters before standing up to speak. This quickly passes when one is certain one has mastered the subject matter beforehand and is "warmed up."

Because of the initial awkwardness in the moments while speaker and audience are "tuning in" to each other, some speakers like to open with an anecdote or humorous story. This can be effective if the story makes a point and serves as an introduction to the topic. Yet some persons who can never tell a story effectively are excellent speakers. Some "amateurs" are very effective because their sincerity and their content command sympathetic listening.

Here are some guidelines found useful for speakers:

- Make certain you understand the nature of the program and of the audience so that you can make your talk appropriate.

- Unless assigned a topic, pick a subject with which you are familiar so that you can talk about personal experiences and observations. Clear with the program director and determine the time allotted to you. For most speakers twenty to thirty minutes should be adequate.

- Be sure you know your subject thoroughly. If you are not familiar with certain areas of the topic, you will need to do some research—by calling or talking with people who do, or by extensive reading and note-taking. Most confident speakers are those who are "filled with their subjects" to the point where they would never run out of material.

- Make an outline of points to be covered with sub-topics for each point.
- Write out your talk, relating your subject to your audience's interest and concerns. Provide an opening to set the stage for the body of the talk and a conclusion to nail down the impression you wish to leave. Keep in conversational vein unless inappropriate for the occasion.
- At this point you may wish to check in your library what others have said on the same topic to make certain you are making your own individual contribution.
- Print each point to be made on a separate card in large enough letters so that you can read it at a glance. Often a few key words are all that are necessary. A felt pen is good for this purpose. Yellow cards with black ink provide the best contrast for visibility. Number cards in order to be given.
- Rehearse your talk by speaking from the cards only, and time your delivery. Turn over each card as point is completed and proceed to next number. As you repeat your delivery, you will probably cut down your time and eliminate points which seem less important.

Experienced speakers sometimes prefer to read a speech. The prepared text assures them that they will say exactly what they intend to say if the subject is a sensitive one and that they can keep to planned time limits. They may read from a typed manuscript on soft paper which will not make rustling noises before the loudspeaker microphone. These are usually in large type of a special typewriter used for speech typing only. Or the speech may be prepared for monitors which are visible to the speaker and invisible to the audience. These are usually for the most formal occasions.

Average speakers will perhaps find the card system more effective since it enables them to be informal, to phrase each point as they "feel" it at the moment of delivery. When not limited by a prepared text, they can take advantage of developments of the occasion—a remark of the master of ceremonies, a comment by a previous speaker, something overheard before the meeting started or during dinner. Any such effort to meet an audience half way establishes rapport and better communication.

Most dangerous to non-professional speakers is getting "off

the subject" and rambling on without regard to time. The audience will be apt to become bored. Speakers can avoid this by rehearsals before a friendly critic and by remembering that deviations must be brief.

Audiences like enthusiasm, human interest, and narrative with a point. They appreciate a liveliness in delivery, but not everyone can adopt such a style. The best substitute is brevity—to get to the point, deliver the message, and stop.

Yet there are exceptions: One man with a hesitation to his speech which seemed always to verge on stuttering kept audiences hanging on his every word. He used his handicap as an asset not to gain audience sympathy, but with humor and grace, which kept them wondering, "What next?"

Need a Speakers Bureau?

When an agency's message requires substantial explanation and there is need to communicate with many groups, a speakers bureau may be considered. Officers, committee chairpersons, staff associates and others may be called upon to speak before various organizations on their own aspects of the agency's work. Or the agency may have a theme which it wishes to bring widely to people's attention and draft as many members as possible for the campaign.

Medical societies, for example, have at certain times become concerned about aspects of child health and called on physician members to speak to parents' organizations, school nurses and teachers. If the people are professionals or specialists, unaccustomed to public speaking, some training and briefing may be necessary before offering them in this capacity. The point is: Some doctors, for example, may know their subject well and be able to communicate with others of their profession, yet be less able to express themselves in popular language. Other professionals are also guilty at times of talking over people's heads.

Training courses for speakers are plentiful, also books and manuals. But for those unable to attend such courses, it is well to screen your speakers before sending them out to represent the organization. A trial run might be a talk before some inside group at which the speaker's effectiveness can be quietly and diplomatically evaluated.

In a city or smaller community, a speaker's bureau may

place speakers before luncheon clubs, women's clubs, civic organizations, church and fraternal groups. Announcements can be made in the press and by mail. Don't overlook radio and television interviews as a way to place your organization in the forefront. For the latter you will need speakers on a variety of subject areas so that one can fit into the broadcast station's programming need at any time.

All speakers should be able to answer questions as well as give a set speech. For this, briefing and background documentation may be necessary to make certain they are prepared for the unexpected.

Building a reputation for providing good speakers takes time. Some organizations prepare their programs a year in advance, so you need to offer speakers well ahead. But if you have speakers ready at a moment's notice when some scheduled speaker cancels out, you may save the program director embarrassment. This wins friends and readier bookings.

Unless managed and promoted by someone who makes a major effort, volunteer speakers bureaus tend to languish after the early enthusiasm wears off. Bookings are slow in coming. The initial crusade falters. Busy professional people find the extra work too great a burden. A particularly able speaker's family needs his attention and leisure time. Yet a few will enjoy this service and be glad to continue in it. If they are capable communicators, are continually challenged with new types of assignments yet not over-exposed, their services can be invaluable in creating an image of the institution and a wider understanding of its concerns and services to the community.

CHAPTER X

WRITING TO COMMUNICATE

In writing it is well to have one's purpose clearly in mind before setting words to paper. Not all writing is for the purpose of communicating, that is, conveying information or knowledge. People write to express feelings, to entertain, to arouse emotional attitudes in others, to persuade to a point of view, or to incite to action.

In contemporary use, the word **communication** often takes on the broader implications of cultivating relationships, as in public relations, employee relations, or community relations, of which communication is a principal part. Or, it may encompass urgency to act, as in promotion and advertising. Communicative writing may also use entertainment as a device for securing attention, but peripherally to the main objective.

Written communication has several advantages which the spoken word alone does not: a permanent record easily copied for wide dissemination; a reminder for the follow-up file of future actions required; a means of settling arguments when memories fail to agree. It has appeal to people who are visually minded, who need to study something before they can fully comprehend it. These are considerations when one is deciding whether or not to communicate by writing.

Style and format of writing varies widely with the medium. But, essentially, there are two types: writing to be read silently, and writing to be read aloud, sometimes known as speech writing or speakwriting.

Writing to Be Read Aloud

In contrast with copy to be read silently to one's self, writing which is to be read aloud may well begin at the beginning in sequence of time or thought and lead logically to the conclusion or climax. Both types of writing must seek to capture attention at the start, but a speaker can be more relaxed. He or she has a captive audience and does not have to worry about listeners' turning the page to something else as a reader might. For the first few minutes, at least, the audience will give expectant attention before deciding to think about something else or to day dream.

Thus in speakwriting, one can open with one's own first awareness of a subject and share with listeners a "voyage of discovery." In presenting a report to the staff, for example, you can review the problem as you first found it, then state the alternate courses you considered, and finally offer the reasoning by which you arrived at the conclusion with which you hope they will agree. You include them in your experiences.

For preparing a talk you expect to deliver yourself, you may find it helpful to assemble your notes in order, then dictate the talk into a recording device from which a stenographer can transcribe it. For some persons this has the advantage of enabling them to be more conversational in words and style than the stilted literary English of their school compositions.

Whether you, or someone else, will deliver the talk, it is well to have a first draft typed rough in triple-spaces, leaving plenty of margins for editing and writing in changes. This enables you to see how your ideas are working out—to approach your copy free from the throes of composition, more in the mood of a listener.

Writing a text for someone else to deliver introduces a new element: the personality of the speaker. What is his or her natural way of speaking? One of the first things to do is to become acquainted with the speaker's style and personality. Does he/she speak rapidly, or deliberately? What kinds of words does he/she use? Can he/she ad lib stories and asides, or will you have to write them in the copy? (Unless the occasion is a formal one, this kind of self-interruption or by-play may be necessary to establish audience rapport.) Does the speaker have any specific preferences or taboos?

When a speech writer sits down at tape recorder or typewriter to begin a speech text, it is normal to bring to mind all he/she has been able to learn about the audience and the occasion. Imagine yourself there, think of the people who will be there as individuals, if possible, then write as you envision their faces, so they will listen and understand.

When writing someone else's text, one places one's self in the character of the speaker in much the same way as an actor assumes a part. Thus the creative task becomes an instinctive, as well as intellectual, exercise for the writer who has thoroughly researched speaker and audiences, as well as the topic of discussion.

Writing a speech, even more than other writing, seems to require freedom from interruption. Don't worry about editing at first—the unfinished sentences or incomplete ideas. Just get it down on paper or tape. At this point you are concerned about ideas and style, not grammar or perfection. Primarily, you are interested in orchestration—rhythm and flow of thoughts which will capture and carry an audience's attention from beginning to end.

If at first you can't find an appropriate opening, skip it, and write down the body of the speech, step by step, adding a conclusion that sums up your objective. When you have concluded, re-read to see if it really adds up—that you haven't omitted anything essential. Then put it away for a time.

For most people, editing and creativity require different mind sets. Some people do edit as they write, but write more slowly —perhaps logically, but often without enthusiasm and fire. Editing requires that one put one's self mentally in the audience, look at the copy from their point of view, and imagine how they will react.

When the final text is to be prepared, instruct the typist to make wide margins and short lines. A line of text should be comprehensible to the speaker at a glance. Margins provide space for speaker's notations in the event he/she wants to emphasize a point or ad lib a story.

Where available, a typewriter with "speech type" is desirable, otherwise the largest typewriter face available should be used in triple or quadruple space. For organizations which have many formal occasions for speeches, such a special typewriter may be worth while—or projection prompters invisible to the audience, of a type used for television broadcasts.

Unless slides are used, or other visual device, it is well, in writing a talk, to remember that statistics will not be remembered unless simply and dramatically presented. Use round numbers, and sparingly. Use plentiful illustrations and incidents to compensate for what the audience cannot see. Where facts are too overwhelming for memories, strive to help people retain meaningful impressions, even when they cannot recall details.

In writing a speech, one danger is to be carried away with the sound of words and forget the substance of your message. Your purpose is to communicate, or to involve people emotionally in your agency's problems, let's say. You want them afterward to comment, not "That was a good talk," but "What a wonderful job his/her organization is doing!"

On one occasion a Rotary Club speaker had his audience tremendously excited and enthused by witty phrases and oratorical rhetoric; but the author, then a reporter, could find no substance in his talk worth reporting in a news story. On another occasion a farmer, untrained in speaking, held a large audience of clergymen and laymen absorbed and quietly moved by a simple recital of his own personal experiences which he found of religious significance for everyday living.

Research and Preparation

Unless one is knowledgeable in a subject, the research may well take much longer than the writing. The author was once assigned the task of writing a basic guide to selecting a vocation, preparing for it, locating a job and succeeding in the job. Once the purpose and general theme were agreed upon, the research and organization of material took three weeks; the writing, less than three days of dictation to a stenographer.

An executive with training in the military had a formula for every task:
        a. analyze
        b. organize
        c. systematize
        d. deputize

With some adaptation, this formula can be applied to communication problems. In writing, you might apply it in this way:

* **Analyze.** Write down all factors which must be considered in preparing your communication: the occasion or reason for it; the audience or readership it will reach; their knowledge of the subject and comprehension level; their attitudes toward the subject both favorable and unfavorable; how the concerns

and interests of your organization parallel theirs; the aspects you must stress to secure their agreement, action or whatever your objective may be. Assemble all available facts and illustrations to support these.

* **Organize** the material. Print each point or idea to be used on a separate 3 x 5 card or slip of paper. Sort in order to be presented with attention to logical progression and sustained interest. Type rough outline based on these headings, leaving room for subheadings to be added. Insert on cards or in the outline indication of how each main point will be supported—past experience, national statistics, case stories, third person testimony, and the like.

Research further—in the literature or with others who are knowledgeable. If you will speak about an agency program, discuss details with person in charge and others involved in it. Get examples of how it works in operation, what it does for the participants, human interest stories of those helped by it. Put each story on a separate card or slip of paper, easier for organization later when you write.

* **Systematize.** This applies especially where a talk is to be given to a number of audiences, as, for example, when you are booked into all community service clubs to tell about a new program your agency is launching. List all the conditions necessary for an effective presentation—the flip-over chart; slides, projector and screen, extension cord; or other audio-visual assists. Perhaps you will need an assistant to handle the equipment. Make a check list, noting any special arrangements which host should know about in advance, and time needed for on-the-spot setup. Note any gestures or stage business which adds to effectiveness. (You may pick up ideas each time you give the talk.) So-called "natural" speakers may need none of this, but put over their message by sheer subject knowledge and personality. But they are few. For most of us successful speeches are the result of rehearsal with endless attention to details which work and avoidance of those which distract.

* **Deputize.** Success of most speakers depends also on help and cooperation of others: The typist who puts the text in convenient form, the host who makes necessary arrangements, the master of ceremonies who gives you an introduction that starts you off on the right footing, your assistant who operates the a-v

equipment. In turning over these responsibilities, two things are necessary—clear instructions, preferably in writing so that they cannot be overlooked or forgotten, and re-checking.

Even with the most careful precautions, something can go wrong. So try to anticipate. Is the room too big for the size screen you usually use? Is the microphone working? Has anyone thought to place a rug across your power extension cord at a traffic point so no one will kick it loose from the socket at a crucial point? The list is endless. The introduction, if witty, may set the wrong audience attitude for a serious, even ominous report. Give your master of ceremonies information and guidance on this.

Cliche introductions tell what an important and successful person the speaker is. There are occasions where this is appropriate. But, often, a better introduction would be a statement about the subject and why it is important to the particular audience. If the mayor is speaking to the Rotary Club about a proposed program to modernize the street lighting, its members don't need to know about his well-publicized achievements. Before hearing the mayor tell how it should reduce crime, they do need to realize the dimensions of the problem locally. The mayor might well indicate to the Rotary president that he plans to give many details about muggings, burglaries of businesses, accidents in poorly lighted traffic areas, and the like. But he might also suggest that an appropriate introduction would be mention of any Rotarians affected by such problems and the importance of the problem to all its members.

Someone has written a "law" that "If anything can go wrong, it will." This is particularly true of speeches. The speech writer may well prepare the speaker for this with a suggested witticism for the occasion. In any case, a speaker should be prepared mentally for just such a happening. The speaker whose opening establishes rapport and a sense of communication with his audience is not likely to lose them because something does not go smoothly. Many good speakers turn these occasions to advantage, arousing audience's sympathy and admiration by their own refusal to get upset or let accidents come between them.

Writing to Be Read Silently

Organization of material is doubly important with the silent reader. If a speaker's opening is weak, he has a captive audience and may get a second chance to capture their full attention. In contrast, a reader who finds an opening paragraph uninteresting, may turn to something else. That is why newspaper stories tell the "who, what, why, when, where and how" in a first paragraph or two. That persuades advertising writers to keep their copy short and to use dramatic headlines.

In one popular magazine, most articles put the reader "on scene" in the first paragraph preferably in the opening sentence. To a one-time editor of this publication, an ideal opening sentence was: "The plant superintendent and the chief steward strode down the executive corridor and burst into the president's office."

This graphic opening of an article on labor-management relations took the reader at once into the midst of the action. It showed the conflicting personalities and the place where disputes were settled. It provided a cliff-hanger which kept the reader in suspense and eager to learn more.

Most written communications will not need to open so dramatically. For example, one common form—the report—may assume that the readers already are aware of the problem and open with the conclusion its authors have reached. Management often demands that written reports be made succinct—not more than a single page of statement—although much supporting data may be attached. The reason is the great volume of reading an executive must do and the need to conserve his/her time.

Some managements require that a report state all the alternate solutions for a problem with the detailed advantages and disadvantages of each, leaving the decision to be made at management top level. Others ask for this full review, but with the investigator's own preferred solution indicated. In making an assignment an executive may well state his preference, depending on the importance he attaches to the project and the trust he places in his investigator's judgment.

Sometimes for strategic reasons, an executive may direct the one making the report to present it in a particular form for circulation to a board or special committee. A C.E. may know the impatience of a key board member, for example, with intricate, printed explanation and his/her need to have a matter capsulized before confirming a first impression with endless verbal questions later.

To mention honesty in preparing a communication may seem redundant. But honesty goes beyond accuracy, important as correct factual information is. Even in communicating verbally person to person, how easy it is sometimes to be completely misunderstood! Yet, face to face discussion eventually makes it evident when someone has misinterpreted your intention or meaning. In written communication, there is no opportunity for observing the fleeting expression or change of mood which indicates disagreement or dissatisfaction. To be credible, understood and accepted, one must:

- Check and re-check facts and the statement of them.

- Avoid language with double meaning or vague terms open to more than one interpretation.

- Use language and language level which persons reading it comprehend.

- Write lean copy—free of unneeded adjectives and adverbs, in simple sentences, using active verbs and crisp nouns of few syllables. Keep subject matter unequivocal and uncomplicated. Experts have devised formulas with point systems for judging any copy's level of communication. These are mostly useful when learning to write for the general public. They give a good check on whether your writing is geared to the average newspaper reader but would be inappropriate to preparation of a paper for a scientific or other professional group.

When the objective of writing is to inform or to educate, rather than to entertain, persuade or move people to action—success can be measured by whether the two or more persons involved come to a shared understanding of a situation. Although they may approach the situation with different attitudes because of their backgrounds, shared understanding often provides a beginning for working out an agreement or compromise.

But much of modern communication has some further objective: To persuade someone to a point of view or to exhort them to take some action. This may call for adding emotion to facts and ideas.

Writing Persuasively

In some instances it is possible to persuade people to a point of view by sheer weight of facts and other evidence. Suppose your objective is to persuade a parent that it is desirable to send her daughter to your camp. She will be reassured by your document listing your camp's safety record, the calibre and training of its staff, the descriptions of courses and activities ensuring a daughter's growth and development, the pictures of the facilities in use with healthy, happy youngsters enjoying them.

These may persuade the mother to apply for her daughter's admission, but probably not without one additional bit of evidence: third person testimony. Before she entrusts her daughter's welfare to your people, she will probably need to hear the enthusiastic comments of another mother about her daughter's experiences the previous year. Such a comment quoted in writing a promotional announcement, if the person quoted is well known, often carries great weight.

Assembling a weight of evidence may persuade some to change their point of view, but not necessarily. A salesman, on one occasion, out-talked and out-argued his customer on every point. When he had departed, the prospect remarked, "He won the argument, but he lost a sale." Like this customer, many people possess a "gut feeling" that, despite the evidence, the conclusion is wrong. An alert salesman would have sensed that his assumption about the customer's business was in error and pressed for feedback information.

In writing to persuade, one must make doubly certain that one's assumptions about prospects are correct, for printing and mailing costs make errors expensive. Also, feedback is slow in arriving, and lost time in finding out may be vital. With camp season a few weeks away, failure in communication can be disastrous. Where involving emotional appeal, it is well to check proposed copy with several representative prospects before finalizing it.

How does one write persuasively? Enthusiasm is one key. When sincere, it is often contagious. But whose enthusiasm? What kind of enthusiasm? As promoter of the program, your enthusiasm may be suspect. But the enthusiasm of another mother or last year's camp participant could be persuasive. Enthusiasm of teachers who have observed what a camp program did for a youngster is excellent evidence. Often it is well to put such testimony into a letter of transmittal rather than an information folder. This makes it more personal, even though the letter may be a reproduced form.

Writing to persuade must appeal to the other's personal interests. Whether in a single letter to a prospect or in a broadside appeal, the more you can learn of the recipients' needs, the more you can show them how your offer can help satisfy those needs. The more needs to which you can appeal in a printed communication, the more responses you are likely to receive. Advertisers have used this knowledge effectively in selling products; agencies can use the same in offering services and enlisting support for community betterment.

Those who write much promotional copy may find it worth while to review Maslow's studies of human needs and how they cause people to act. (See Chapter VI.) Communication-to-persuade offers its readers something in return for an action requested. It may be **explicit**—money, a certificate of achievement, admission to a group, a name on a building—or **implicit**—recognition by peers, satisfaction of doing something worth while to help fellow citizens, or preservation of their memory long after death.

Sometimes the persuasiveness is negative—implied loss through failure to act. Best prospects for volunteers for the cancer drive are relatives of victims of the disease who know its horrors and want to remove this threat from their own and others' lives. These are already knowledgeable and motivated. In other cases, educational communication may be necessary. Statistics of growing incidence of cancer and case histories of its injury to others may be necessary to create a sense of urgency in asking for help.

Much persuasive writing is based on the appeal of implied future reward. Brokers, politicians and clergymen know this well, although their "rewards" differ widely. This non-material medium of exchange—hope—is potent, but must be used discreetly. Promises must not be made which cannot be fulfilled, or for which resources are not available and authorized. Many troubles in the social agency field have arisen because of over-enthusiastic and over-optimistic observations which raised people's expectations beyond any realistic hope of fulfillment.

Most persuasive communications should have a cut-off date.

Unless a promotion carries a date after which applications will no longer be received—or registration fee increased—or benefits reduced, the communication lacks a sense of urgency. It is easy for a prospect to put off making a decision and responding until he/she has forgotten the whole matter. The ideal is to catch someone in the first burst of enthusiasm by urging a "return mail" response because of limited facilities and a first-come, first-served policy. Of course, if this is not true, such copy can backfire—a prospect may sense the falsity and be turned off, or have need to postpone a decision and later fail to respond through believing it is too late.

Where no sense of urgency exists, it may be necessary to create one. Fund raisers have learned this lesson well. They have introduced progressive goals for annual drives with report dates for competing teams in first period, second period, etc. They have induced large donors to offer matching grants for limited times only. Similar tactics can be introduced into membership drives, program offerings, and drives for volunteers. The point is to set attainable goals and then write promotional copy which will persuade others to want, and to act, to see them attained—on time.

CHAPTER XI

USING PICTURES FOR IMPACT

For best results, there is no communication like showing. Next best to having people see a program in operation is to picture it for them. Your appeal for contributions to send boys or girls from less privileged families to summer camp will get more favorable attention when photographs illustrate your point.

Films used in schools and business training, also television in the homes, have created a generation that wants to be shown, not told. Somewhat earlier, teachers effectively used drawings, diagrams, cross-sectional projections, photos, models and mockups to increase interest and comprehension in the classroom. Even senior citizens will respond more readily to a folder which shows their peers in action.

Yet, in our audio-visual age, inflation of communication activites has caused great competition for readers' attention. Communicators must strive ever harder to achieve the same impact as in the past. While an individual picture may no longer, as was once said, be "worth ten thousand words," the value of words has also been reduced by excess.

Put Life in Your Illustrations

For these reasons, every chief executive or public relations specialist learns to make pictures and text more mutually supportive, with both directly focused on a clearly defined objective. Here are a few guidelines for effective picture communication:

• Use people in photographs. Impressive buildings and facilities may appeal to architects and purchasing agents. But when you are appealing to members, contributors, program prospects, or parents, you'll need to show people using them to make a most favorable impression. To compel attention and persuade readers, you require pictures of persons with whom they can identify or for whom they feel instant concern. Buildings and facilities are not objectives, but means to objectives which must be expressed in terms of people.

- **Get action in your photos.** People posing are rarely as interesting as people who are busy. Senior citizens around a bridge table might be a depressing picture, unless the photographer catches the absorbed concentration in the faces of the competitors—or the joy of triumph over a winning hand contrasted with rueful faces of losing opponents.

Imagine a photo of your camp's lake with canoes, rafts and diving boards waiting for the season to begin—then contrast with pictures of boys having fun—racing to be first in the water or engaged in canoe-tilting competition! Picture girls or boys learning skills—making craft items, such as in ceramics, carpentry, weaving, or leatherwork—or growing in maturity as they relate to understanding counselors as teachers.

- **Catch "candids" when possible.** Except for trained actors under professional directors, people are seldom as convincing photographically, or as interesting, as when they are caught doing what comes naturally. If you must pose people, once they are ready, try fussing with your camera to throw them off guard and let them relax. Then snap them before they think you are ready. Alternately, take an extra shot after they think you are through and they become unposed.

- **Take closeups.** Faces can often convey emotion that takes your communication beyond information to involvement.

- **Show what readers want to see.** Parents want to be certain their youngsters will be happy at your youth programs. Pictures of other youngsters enjoying themselves may help persuade them. They want to know the quality of your personnel; photos of your nurse or a counselor demonstrating their concern for a teen-ager's problem provide some of the evidence they need.

- **Use cartoon animals or birds in place of people.** Drawings are desirable where a photograph is unavailable or where the idea is of paramount importance. For a resource where illustrations are needed quickly without time to obtain a photograph, subscribe to a cartoon clip service. Animals and children have always been popular picture subjects. As an art gallery proprietor has observed, "Pictures with people or animals always sell faster."

• **Use artist's drawings.** Where no appropriate photo is available to illustrate a point, order a drawing for your purpose. In communities without commercial art studios, a high school art student or teacher may be found who will do this. Communicators using many illustrations will find it desirable to tear especially effective ones from advertisements and magazines to stimulate ideas for future use. These may also be used on posters and bulletin boards with your own captions when appropriate to an idea you want to convey.

Eliminate the Negative and the Distracting

• **Avoid distracting details.** Too many extraneous elements reduce a picture's impact. If impossible to eliminate non-essential background in taking or printing a photo, crop closely to make sure your main point is not lost.

• **Anticipate negative impressions.** Consider whether your pictures could cause a problem through under-representation of some ethnic group. Where photos emphasizing inclusion of minorities may be lacking, you may make the point by using drawings rather than photos as illustrations.

• **Use charts and graphs.** Anyone can put together simple bar or line charts with a sheet of white paper, a ruler, a drawing pen, and India ink. Often better than many words, such a chart can show relationships—growth from previous years, or a growing demand-cost squeeze on resources. These provide the ultimate in reducing a fact to its simplest form for major impact.

• **Introduce the unusual.** Imagination and a sense of humor can add interest to an illustration. People tire of cliche photos, such as a company representative presenting a $50,000 check to the chairman of your building fund. One public relations professional had the idea of taking a closeup of the check with a hand signing it. Checks pictured in newspapers can seldom be read, even if held toward the camera face out. Another company had a check blown up to a size of six feet long. Properly signed by the company officials, it was presented at the bank and actually cashed. This offered a number of picture possibilities in addition to the standard one of the company official presenting it to the drive chairman. And it could be read when reproduced in the local newspaper!

Focus On the Idea

Every illustration begins with an idea. Unless a picture communicates that idea, it is of little use. It must get across the idea interestingly, or it may fail to capture readers' attention.

Here is how a good professional news photographer earns his salary. He looks for faces with expression and personality, for a different angle—bird's eye view of a softball competition or worm's eye view of a child with a pet—for the unusual subjects or for an off-guard moment. He strives for a new way of looking at something as well as to make a point. He may frame one youngster who is his main subject by two of his fellows, shooting between them. Or he may surround the child with objects which suggest the nature of his environment.

When you employ a photographer to take your program illustrations, or assign the task to a talented volunteer, explain what message you hope to convey. Sometimes writing brief captions in advance helps: Camp Wildwood Develops Character. Senior Citizens Discover New Usefulness as Foster Grandparents. With this kind of guidance, your photographer may produce photos which need little or no explanation.

Pictures, like text, must be honest. Photos may not lie, yet misrepresent. One person in the crowd doing something forbidden in your activities may give a wrong impression which will be difficult to erase. One practical joker can ruin a group shot. These off-beat details must be constantly sighted and avoided. No picture at all is better than a bad one. Before final use, each picture must be carefully examined for total impact.

Captions That Capture Interest

Captions should be terse and provide any necessary clues to understanding what a picture is saying. One mistake made by some caption writers is to repeat in words what is already obvious from the photo. Essential to a caption may be identification of persons in a picture, location of the subject matter and when taken. In other instances these may be distracting.

Headline captions are sometimes used above a photo or above the text beneath a photo. These are usually one-liners in capital letters in contrast with text captions which may extend to several lines. Photos ideally catch the eye and the attention of a reader, but headline captions should excite his/her interest to look longer for more detail and to read the text.

When your objective is communication, try to think what information or impression you want the reader to gain and retain from looking at this picture. Then try to capsulize that in a word or phrase which can be included in the headline.

Suppose your children's day camp stages a mock circus and your photo shows two or three in clown suits in a tumbling act as parents watch from the sidelines. A headline caption might be: MORE FUN THAN A CIRCUS AT CAMP WILDWOOD. The pun attracts attention; it says youngsters enjoy themselves; and it identifies the camp. The photo reinforces this message and further identifies satisfied parents. If the headline is too long for the photo, shorten it to: CAMP LIFE'S A CIRCUS! This does not get the name in headline, but conveys the message.

Using Pictures in Series

When using more than one picture, there are several considerations to remember. Anyone who will face this task will do well to consult a good book on picture layouts. Let's say you have the pictures from last year's harvest festival and are ready to prepare a folder promoting this year's benefit. The photographer has followed your instructions of ideas to illustrate, and you have a nice variety of photos from which to select.

Start with the ideas. Put pictures which illustrate the same idea together in piles. Now you have your choices before you. Begin with the first idea you will present—perhaps a distance shot of a colorful row of booths, or a costume dance a keynote picture which illustrates what the festival is all about for the cover. This may be a difficult choice—you like the action of the dancers; on the other hand, you know that, for many, the bargains in the booths may be the big attraction. Since it is a family occasion, you may finally remember the great attraction of youngsters and animals and settle for a close-up of a child with a dog in the pet competition, with judges looking on.

Perhaps you will decide that the cover calls for a montage of pictures showing the variety of events and appeals of your festival. This requires other considerations: interspersing exciting action with more quiet pictures for contrast; making certain that tone values of the pictures do not clash; avoiding composition that leads the eye off the page instead of back toward the next picture. But whatever your cover, you will want it to excite the reader's interest to turn inside.

Select the best picture from each pile devoted to an idea. Ask whether it really tells the story. Is it a good photo for reproduction? Is it interesting to you? If it whets your interest, it should appeal to others.

Place your selections roughly in order on a large table or the floor. Now ask yourself whether interest flows naturally from each to the next. Is there too much similarity in subject matter or composition? If so, you may need to go back to a pile and substitute a second best picture in the interest of effectiveness of the whole. Does it all—with the text you will add—communicate what you intended from the beginning? As to arrangement, do the picture compositions lead the eye naturally to the next in each case? (One notable danger is a close-up profile facing off a page. In such cases, have a reverse print made.) Sometimes arrows or other artificial devices are helpful where eye direction is important.

At times it is desirable to **use a photo story**—tell something in a series of photographs much as you would film action in a movie. These are usually arranged thus: a large photo with a lead paragraph of the story, then smaller pictures left to right in sequence and text captions carrying on the narrative. These could occupy a center spread of a folder. Each individual picture must add something new to the reader's information.

At times it is more effective to key **the photographs with numbers** on the photos and in the text, letting the story continue as a mass of type rather than be broken up for lines under each photo. This is especially true where more explanation may be needed for some pictures than others.

Another type layout is the **wheel or frame.** The text is placed in the center and numbered pictures surround it. This is much used for portraits of people in a story where little action is pictured.

Using different layouts from time to time is attention-compelling. But the final test is whether they achieve your stated objective. To paraphrase comedian-philosopher Flip Wilson: What **they** see is what **you** get across to others. Good visuals are good communication.

CHAPTER XII

HIGH PRIORITY COMMUNICATION

An executive who neglects communication with any of his/her organization's constituencies is courting trouble. That is why it is essential to take time periodically—away from pressing administrative problems and the interruptions of telephone, visitors, and meeting obligations—to review the total communication effort.

This is especially important for communication with insider groups—those persons who have invested time, money and dedicated service in the institution. They have a proprietary interest in everything that affects its welfare. They count on the chief executive to keep them informed of every major development and spare them the embarrassment of hearing such news from some outside source.

With this "in-group," being among the first to know is a matter of pride. The C.E. who ignores one of this core group, however innocently, in pushing a proposal may find he/she has created an opponent and trouble for the project. Or, the person may withdraw in a huff and look elsewhere for a "cause."

Assigning Communication Priorities

First important thing for a chief executive is to determine communication priorities. Certainly, highest priority must be given to members of the governing board, especially the chairperson and other key members. The chairperson may need filling in on a daily or weekly basis depending on the pace of events. Others with high priorities, including key and long-service staff and volunteers, must be briefed according to their interests and involvement.

On a continuing but less frequent basis high priority communication will include large financial donors: individual donors, foundation executives, heads of contributing corporations and United Way. Not to be forgotten are prospects whose interest is being cultivated.

Once the C.E. establishes who rate high priority communication, the next step is to determine exactly what the communication objective is in each case. With one person it may be to increase the size of an annual gift, with another to persuade him/her to accept a committee chairmanship. With all, there will be a need to keep them interested, involved and supportive. An overall objective will be to keep everyone working in the same direction for the organization's long- and short-range goals.

Creating Unity of Board and Staff

Getting everyone within and without an institution to view it in the same light—to possess the same image of it and its objectives—is sometimes difficult. Failure in communication can result in disagreements within the board, in staff failure to carry out policies and follow guidelines due to differing interpretations or preconceptions, and in confusion among the volunteer leadership. Unless major differences are first resolved at the board level, communication with the others can hardly be clear and effective.

Of course, a great contribution to unity begins with selection of board members. People should be avoided who seek to use the organization for their own purposes—publicity, political advancement, non-related objectives—generally those who seek membership rather than wait to be asked. What is needed are dedicated, concerned people with no personal "axes to grind," who have the community's welfare at heart and are capable of contributing to problem-solving. But in practice, every C.E. works with imperfect people and seeks through communication to provide them with premises for judgment and action.

In a busy society, assembling a governing board is often difficult. One agency executive in this situation finds no substitute for person-to-person communication. He meets with small committees or individuals, spends much time on the telephone, not only during office hours but also evenings and weekends.

This man begins with new members before they join the board. He finds reasons for joining are often personal, unrelated to his organization's primary objectives. Some join for social reasons because their friends are members, others because of the prestige membership brings in certain interest groups. Now and then a new member has a specific project which he/she hopes to "sell" to the institution.

A new member who joins with a mistaken image of the organization can be disruptive with comments at the first meeting attended, resulting in embarrassment to all concerned. To prevent this, the chief executive makes an appointment during the first month after his/her election.

During this get-acquainted session, the C.E. outlines the organization's policies, objectives and programs and supplies material on its past and present activities. He attempts by this educational process to get the new board member to share the others' outlook. (See Chapter III).

A New Trustee's Education

One newly appointed trustee of this institution—a Jewish Family Center—was an elderly member of the community greatly concerned about the need for education of the younger generations in Jewish culture and traditions. As always, the C.E. probed for his reason for accepting membership on the Board of Trustees. It soon became apparent that his chief purpose was to sell the center a program of classes on Jewish heritage for youngsters.

After listening at some length to the man's concern, the C.E. diplomatically pointed out programs already available in the community along these lines in other institutions. He was also able to get the man to see that his proposal would require major changes in the policies and goals of the center, as well as substantial addition of facilities and financing.

The center's purpose was to provide recreation for the entire family, the C.E. noted. It was for this that the members joined and paid dues which now kept the institution in operation. The facilities were geared to physical fitness and recreational activities and were now fully used, he explained. No space was suitable for classrooms.

Was the new trustee certain that the need was greater for such cultural instruction than other institutions were already prepared to supply? If so, what did he think about the willingness of the community to finance a major building program and to pay fees to support instructional overhead? Would he, for example, be interested in heading a fund-raising committee and contribute substantially toward such a project?

With such questions, he was able to help the man see that his idea should certainly not be introduced lightly into a governing board discussion and that perhaps he had chosen the wrong organization for his proposal.

Listening sympathetically can be a strong communication asset. Enthusiasm in a supporter is to be encouraged. One who comes up with an idea needs an attentive ear and deserves thoughtful consideration. Even those ideas which at first seem impractical may have some merit and with some modification may be incorporated in a project, thereby enlisting the originator's support and enthusiasm in working toward organizational goals.

Board Chairperson as Key Communicator

Central to communication with the trustees is the leadership role of the presiding officer. As a hired employee, the chief executive cannot inform a board member that his comments at a board meeting are irrelevant. But the chairperson, exercising his/her responsibility, can declare them out of order, pointing out that they are straying from the subject, or from the meeting's purpose. He/she can keep members from social conversation until the business in hand is completed.

This dilemma emphasizes the need for an agenda for every meeting. The C.E. mentioned above trains the chairpersons to be strong leaders and presiding officers. Before each meeting, he or she briefs the chairperson on matters likely to come up and offers an agenda which the chairperson usually accepts, securing its adoption at the start. This provides a perfect device for keeping discussion in line so that differing points of view are presented and reconciled for a prompt decision.

The chairperson and chief executive usually come to agreement in advance as to what they hope will come out of the meeting. This enables the chairperson, while permitting full discussion and still allowing for new developments which may change this objective, to steer the members' thinking back toward the hoped-for goal. He or she can invite someone to offer a motion when it is felt there is a chance for a decision.

Because of the C.E.'s constant communication with all members of the board and with others of the key organizational supporters, the chief executive can serve in another valuable role. He/she can keep the chairperson apprised of trustees' attitudes and personalities. As a volunteer, the chairperson needs this kind of briefing in order to serve wisely and effectively. As a listener, the C.E. will be aware of each one's motivations and how they are likely to react in a given situation. A good C.E. should be able to scent trouble ahead and warn the chairperson accordingly.

Systematizing High Priority Communication

Although the chief executive may know all his/her priority people well, communication with them is too important to be left to chance or memory. Especially with organizations that are growing, most C.E.'s will at some point find there are more problems than they can encompass. At such times, they will be grateful if they have set up a system for high priority communication.

The objectives of the system are to ensure that every person important to the organization is advised of every new development ahead of public announcement, that he or she receives all information wanted (and to which that person is entitled).

This may take the form of a master card for each such person with personal information, such as other members of family, notable dates, etc., but with emphasis on fields of interest within the organization. Some C.E.'s keep file folders on each key person with clippings, birth dates for sending cards, hobbies for refreshing the C.E.'s memory just before an important interview and the like. The personal information may prevent a C.E. from mistakenly congratulating a board member on her daughter's graduation from college, for example, when she has just received her doctorate.

But the essential part of the communication file is to remind you that one contributor wants to be kept abreast of the vocational guidance seminars while another is chiefly interested in developments in the day care program. When these areas of interest have been determined, preparation of lists for each subject area (day care, senior seminars, vocational guidance, etc.) can be turned over to a competent assistant, with instructions to send appropriate materials as issued with the C.E.'s card attached and to keep records of what is sent. C.E.'s who have the time will want to initial these personally, perhaps add a few words of comment, depending on the importance of the communication.

Another important record lists the dates of contacts with high priority persons (H.P.P.s). Time goes quickly and without a tickler system for following up communication on some regular basis, a C.E. may suddenly find that he/she has neglected to talk to someone personally for months.

In the beginning, in determining the purpose of contacts with each high priority person, it is well to establish target dates for each objective. These should be realistic. Even so, they may not be attained. For example, your goal is a gift of a half million dollars for a swimming pool from an elderly couple whose athletic daughter began her career in your youth program. You need a series of communication targets or you are not likely to reach this goal.

First, your final target will be to have the gift in hand, the pool completed, so that they can both attend the opening ceremonies and enjoy the result of their generosity. Depending on the state of their health, this gives your project a sense of urgency.

Target dates will include preparation of the case for the pool's construction (the need, cost, and expected benefits of the project); public announcement of the objective; notification of your prime prospects by general announcement; interview to show your prospects what they could do for the community and to prolong their memory after they are gone; followup contacts through their friends.

Other targets may be needed—perhaps involvement of the daughter, their attorney or financial advisor.

All these will take time, and unless a time schedule is set, your campaign may be too late.

Staff Reports and Reporting to the Board

Communication of the highest priority includes reports to the board. The board has the responsibility of making and revising policy. It cannot exercise this function wisely unless it can rely on the information supplied its members. Here's where the executive must use caution and judgment. Accuracy is important, and the C.E. must insist staff members all be realistic in their reports to him/her and not go overboard with enthusiastic optimism.

Of each proposal, board members need to know the amount of dollars needed to buy staff and facilities. They must know the results to be expected and have a goal by which to measure accomplishments. How many volunteers of what quality can be enlisted? In fund-raising, what amounts will a specific effort produce? What could go wrong? What are the risks?

The board needs also to be kept informed as a program progresses. If it fails to work out as planned, it is better to let the members know early rather than find out when it is too late to change the course of events.

A board's decisions will be only as good as its information. Therefore the C.E. must insist on the best reporting—in both quantity and quality—of which his staff members are capable. At the same time, the C.E. is responsible in transmitting their information to evaluate and interpret it. The C.E. best knows the strengths and weaknesses of each staff member and is in position to check their accuracy and question the validity of their claims and projections. Some are better at writing reports than in performance, others more modest than their work would justify. The C.E. can educate them about need for greater objectivity and for realism, or, failing in this, provide board members with additional perspective.

One danger in reporting to the board stems from human frailty. One tends to credit oneself with successes while attributing failures to others or factors beyond one's control. This must be ruthlessly suppressed lest C.E. or staff member fall into a trap. Board members may begin attributing all success to their wisdom and blame the C.E. for failures. A community service organization, like a sports team, is a joint effort. All must share in the joy resulting from a success and credit be passed around liberally. This enables everyone to support each other in times of stress and disappointment.

A Personal Touch in Fund Raising

No major organizational development can be finalized without a consensus among the high priority persons. This is notably true of large financial supporters. One needs to present new ideas and programs to such as unfinished. As with staff members, their enthusiasm grows with their participation in the creative process. Benjamin Franklin noted this in his **Autobiography**. He found that when he offered a new idea of his own, it was better to suggest it with hesitancy, even doubting its merit. This led the other person to avoid criticism, but rather to look for merit in it and to seek to reassure him in his own apparent uncertainty. So with board members and large givers. One who feels "in" at the birth of an idea is likely to be a strong advocate.

When an H.P.P. does present criticism or reservations, it is time to take a second look. Perhaps there is concern that the new idea may lead away from an agency's original objectives. Or the new may appear as a competitor for organizational resources with an established program to which he/she is emotionally committed. In this case the C.E. needs to reassure the H.P.P. by showing how the new can aid in achieving traditional objectives or support an existing effort.

Silence of board members when a proposal is discussed is significant and communication in itself. Chairpersons need to be instructed to bring out an opinion from everyone and to let reservations be expressed. When a large financial donor changes the subject in a personal conversation, an executive should listen carefully. Lack of enthusiastic response may suggest that timing is wrong. There may be a need to find out what is on the other's mind first and save the new proposal for another occasion.

Long-time supporters are generally conservative in their approach to an institution's activities. They have seen old ideas and ways work and may be suspicious of the new. They may be unaware of community changes which make once-dynamic programs anachronisms. Bringing them up to date requires diplomacy and finesse.

Handling Criticisms and Objections

In such situations, one must remember that the objector does not have all the information you have, nor, perhaps, the current personal involvement. For example, a financial supporter or board member who has grown up in a more authoritarian era may feel uncomfortable with the openness and permissiveness in youth programs today. With such, one must begin step-by-step education from personal knowledge, for example, on children of families with working mothers and absent fathers and the extra attention these young people need. With detailed explanation of their previous lack of discipline and oversight, the

H. P. P. may come to understand the need for special programs to help these less privileged catch up.

When hesitancy is based on competition for resources, it may be expected to generate new sources of support and a new clientele for the agency's activities. Estimates based upon studies of need and of supporter interest, together with actual promises of gifts, may be necessary to remove this apprehension.

Sometimes old-timers' objections are based upon previous failures which others have forgotten and which they feel provide lessons in fundamentals. They may be concerned with legal and social difficulties of which a new project's sponsors are unaware. Or they may believe that a new direction in programming will destroy an institutional image carefully built over many years. Whether or not an image change may be needed, such objections are worth a careful hearing, as the following story illustrates.

A Case of Incomplete Listening

At an annual meeting of an organization devoted to health and medical problems affecting women, a younger group of delegates were enthused by International Women's Year and proposed a long resolution condemning the practices of some nations in discriminating against women's health needs. A proposer consulted one of the older members who suggested the idea was good but that a woman attorney present be consulted about the language. The sponsors ignored the advice.

When the resolution came to the floor, it was defeated. The persuasive argument against it came from a long-time delegate and fighter for women's rights. She observed that the resolution was inconsistent with and in violation of, the organization's charter. Her first point was that, although the resolution stated it was non-political, by specifically condemning certain practices which were controversial, approving others, and naming names it became political in nature. She also noted that no relationship between these practices and women's health, the organization's stated objective, was clearly substantiated; that this might jeopardize the institution's tax-exempt status.

Following the floor defeat, the chief opponent offered a modified version of the resolution which met her own objections and it was adopted without opposition.

By listening carefully, rather than hearing what they wanted to hear, the sponsors might have avoided confrontation, loss of face, and the bitterness which developed for a time as the result of incomplete communication. Unity and morale might have been preserved by striving for a consensus.

Dealing With High Priority Prejudice

Sometimes supporters are so emotionally committed to old ways that they are not open to new ideas. Yet, sympathetic listening may discover that the basis for a prejudice is not what it seemed at first. When sensitively handled, the most vocal critic may often be changed to the strongest supporter.

An older white woman, afraid of the new ethnic groups who moved into her neighborhood and annoyed by "noisy children," was nevertheless enlisted in a headstart program as a tutor. The appealing, bright young black youngster to whom she was assigned and the other black youngsters she met in the program proved her fears groundless and she became a strong program supporter. There is no remedy for prejudice like experience.

Communicating to Raise Money

Fund raising, of necessity, assumes highest priority at times. Agency executives may wish that dedicated service to a community would automatically draw enough money to support them. But without a communication program having specific financial goals this seldom happens. Fund-raising techniques are not within the scope of this book, but a few observations about this type of communication may be in order.

With charitable contributions as with money spent for products and services of commercial nature, people want to make certain they receive full value for their dollars. First, they must be assured that the agency's services are needed and wanted by the community and by the clients served. Second, they wish to be sure the gifts are carefully spent, not wasted on administrative overhead which is unneeded. Careful givers look to see the fund-raising costs as a percentage of total gifts and will reject appeals which cost more than 10 to 20%, depending on circumstances.

People also want to feel good about their giving. While they may resist pressure on them to give for a cause for which they are less than enthusiastic, they will be reassured when friends whose opinion they value also give and commend them for giving.

People give for these reasons:

- **They see that a need is immediate and pressing.** The appeal of a baby on one's doorstep is stronger than a starving youngster on a foreign mission field.
- **Because of some personal experience.** A heart attack victim or member of his family is a better prospect for the heart fund appeal.
- **From apprehension.** Fear of cancer leads to wanting to contribute to research to prevent or conquer the disease.
- **Pleasant memories,** such as college or preparatory school days.
- Because "everyone is giving." It is the "in-thing" and they want to be one of the crowd, approved by their peers.
- **Good stewardship.** They feel responsible for intelligent use of their money to produce the most good for the community.
- **Personal satisfaction.** They want to see their name on a building, or to have some permanent place in the community or society which has been important to them—after they are no longer in person able to be a part of it.

Whether in personal, conversational appeals or in mail proposals, the more of these motivations one can include, the better one's chance of success. In personal cultivation, one listens and probes for the individual's own desires and satisfactions to learn what appeal to stress. In broadcast or published appeals one includes as many of the aspects as will interest the widest numbers.

Foundation and government grants are controlled by people with similar motivations but their giving is more sophisticated than most individuals. They set standards and requirements which apply to all giving. Government personnel will be concerned about the breadth of outreach and whether a service is appropriate for all citizens to support through taxes—as well as its voter popularity. A foundation will have in mind the specific objectives of the institution under its charter and its demonstrated performance in working toward those objectives.

A community agency's appeal for broad support will be enhanced by a widely known and favorable image. Continuing newspaper and radio-television accounts of its activities throughout the year create a public awareness of what it is accomplishing for the community. The larger and more active the agency, the more visible its image so that fund appeals have less explaining to do. The annual report then will establish the agency's stewardship during the previous year and project its needs for the future. If the board has determined the kind of image it wants to project in the beginning and the staff has worked to justify that image, the donor can more readily judge its worthiness and be moved to contribute his/her share for its support.

Direct Appeals and the United Way

For many years there was controversy over the growing numbers and variety of appeals for financial support. Donors complained that they could not readily judge the relative merit of claims on their generosity and that continued money appeals became an annoyance. Volunteers protested the duplication of personal and telephone calling in mass appeals. Some agencies complained about inability to gain media attention, that larger sums went to agencies with more dramatic activities and less need. So the United Way came into being.

For larger donors, the United Way had great merit, with its evaluation reviews, standards, a single appeal to consider, a single check to write. Corporations felt more justified in giving to a community-wide effort than to specific charities where their choice might be subject to criticism.

From agencies' viewpoint, the United Way conferred status. Its approval reinforced their individual images with their closer constituencies. It provided a channel to business and union support otherwise denied them.

From the community's standpoint, the United Way led to agency cooperation rather than competition, balanced the flow of funds, and imposed tight budgeting. It also provided a vehicle for enlisting top community leadership in its fund drives.

Counterbalancing these advantages was one sizeable communication disadvantage: The breadth of the appeal made it difficult to show the average giver just how his money was used and how great were the needs. Giving approached the level of a commercial transaction—a fulfillment of community expectation rather than a voluntary expression of concern. Also, in years of economic stress, agencies often found their appropriations from United Way cut back as general giving dropped off.

Much as agency executives might like to have the merit of their year's activities judged by one client, the United Way, with assurance needed support would be forthcoming, they cannot afford a one-client stance. Each agency still needs to build its own constituency by involvement of volunteers, and by a continuing communication with its public through all media.

Selling Need for Overhead

With a large volunteer leadership, an organization sometimes finds a need to justify funding for adequate staff support and overhead. In an organization like the Boy Scouts where money for this must in the large measure come from parents of participants, this is especially the case. The professional planning and organizing which makes the volunteer leaders look good is not always visible to non-participants. Through direct mail, publicity and personal contacts, such organizations keep continually at the task.

One area Boy Scout Council has three such efforts annually: Scout Anniversary Week in February, at opening of camp season, and a direct mailing to sustaining members in autumn. In recession periods when contributions to charity tend to drop, it has found one additional way which greatly boosts its contributions.

As the economy becomes tightened, this council puts increasing emphasis on parent participation. Families then become more willing to forego expensive summer vacation trips and to participate in a son's camp experiences. More fathers seem to find the time to serve in leadership roles. Personal observation provides the best communication. Parents participating in scout or cub pack programs begin to understand better the programs' objectives and staff's efforts to make them effective.

This area council finds "bad times" are the best of times financially. Somehow parents who sell themselves on scouting's value find the means themselves, or the ability to persuade others, to contribute whatever is needed to maintain the overhead.

Keeping in Touch--
A Lesson in Persistence

In a period of communication explosion, agencies find it more difficult than ever to get feedback from mail communication. There is a tendency to become discouraged when after observing all basic rules—good copy and layout, built-in feedback, appeal to reader's own interests—one finds the response unrewarding. Even where there are responses, both favorable and unfavorable, mailings may seem to be unsuccessful in achieving an objective.

A medium-size college hired a professional fund-raising organization to mail out to prospective donors a periodic financial newsletter designed to fit its particular communication needs. After four years the college's managers challenged its effectiveness. The public information personnel could not with certainty point to a single contribution of any size resulting from the newsletter. However, two gifts totaling approximately $20,000 might be attributable to the mailings.

Such questions as these were asked: Shouldn't the cost of $600 per year be saved in view of the depressed economic situation and the financial squeeze the institution was undergoing? Shouldn't they reduce the number of persons receiving it? Wasn't it presumptuous to keep widows of alumni on the mailing list? Fortunately, the administration concluded that the program was soundly conceived and executed, and the cost was small in proportion to other costs and the potential of the mailing's objective.

Several months later, an elderly New York woman called the college and identified herself as the widow of an alumnus. She had read the latest financial newsletter describing the college's needs and the methods by which contributions could be made. She would like to speak to the president. To him she expressed something of her late husband's love for his alma mater and stated her interest in bequeathing the college a sum in the neighborhood of $000,000.

Needless to say, the president at once made a luncheon appointment with her to discuss the matter further. During their conversation, she revealed that a neighbor of hers, also a widow, wanted to do something worth while with her estate. She felt the friend might be persuaded to leave the college a sum in the neighborhood of half again as much. Eventually, the college did receive the two bequests totalling one and one-half million dollars triggered by the modest newsletter. Continuing communication over many years with the alumnus and his widow had eventually led to success.

Communication for Cultivation

High priority communication then is for the purpose of cultivating individuals whose support is important to the institution. Whether the objective is fund raising or recruitment of leaders or unifying the organization in pursuit of its purposes and goals, it needs planning, targeting, monitoring, feedback and evaluation on a systematic basis. These steps provide a checklist for such planning and performance.

- Identify each key person, with interests and motivation.
- Provide reference files for each.
- Set goals or targets, with time segment checks.
- Plan communication, deputizing routine portions where possible.
- Enlist other key persons in cultivation of prospects and donors in planning and in decision-making.
- Train staff in quality reporting and chairperson in keeping all efforts "on target."
- Include high priority persons in general communications.
- Listen well and turn dissenters into supporters.
- Review progress periodically and evaluate efforts.
- Persist in soundly-based programs until communication efforts get results.

CHAPTER XIII

BUILDING GOOD RELATIONSHIPS

Much of the communication profession describes its purposes in terms of building relationships—public relations, employee relations, government relations, community relations, supplier relations, and the like. For upon an organization's relationships with individuals and groups will depend the extent of its support.

Quality of relationships depends both on an agency's performance and upon how that performance is perceived by others. Whether people look upon a community arts council as doing a magnificent job in encouraging young talent and raising the city's cultural standards—or as an elitist group imposing its tastes and preferences upon others—results from how it operates and how it communicates.

Keys to good relationships are mutuality and dialogue. Communication to build good relationships must begin where people are. Arts council members who want to share their love for classical or modern sculpture and painting may need to start with pop or folk art. Educators know the value of the contemporary for introducing the origins of concepts and styles—the pillared county courthouse for a study of Greek architecture and ideas or current events to inspire interest in history. This necessity for starting a dialogue is time consuming, but can lead to true love for culture rather than the grudging support of an opera-attending husband who feels hijacked, for example.

Mutual considerations in dialogue with another group may, of necessity, result in modification of beautifully conceived plans. But this effort to avoid people's feeling imposed upon, rather than grateful, is worthwhile, as has been seen in work with ethnic communities.

Good relations are important to the image of the organization. Relationships with staff and employees—good or bad—become known in the wider community. As pointed out earlier, one national organization whose spokesman advocated better employee relations practices in widely publicized addresses lost much of its credibility as it became known that its own internal practices failed to live up to its advocacy. For this reason, many organizations have an official spokesperson who is knowledgeable of both policies and operations—often chairperson of the board—who communicates with those groups where relations are especially important and delicate.

Maintaining Common Objectives

Good relations with other groups are built upon two communication strategies: starting with shared purposes and experiences and negotiating exchanges of advantages to both parties.

Communication with staff and employees stresses the importance of the organization's work and their part in it because without a shared objective, internal relationships are unlikely to be happy. Exchange of money for their time is only a beginning. As the head of one of America's larger corporations once said, "You can buy a man's time, but you have to earn his loyalty and enthusiasm." Listening to the employee's concerns and showing how his/her personal and professional growth and development can be a by-product of working for the agency's objectives and programs, have become an essential management communication function.

Relationships with suppliers are important to every organization. Getting prompt deliveries and extra service in emergency are vital to a smooth-working program. These depend, of course, on the agency's performance—advance ordering to permit normal time for processing and shipping and prompt payment which saves a supplier costs of borrowing. Equally, it depends on communication which helps you understand the supplier's problems.

One agency which had developed excellent relations with suppliers was accustomed to print many of its program promotion pieces internally. It customarily anticipated its requirements for paper for the year ahead and placed tentative orders well in advance. In tight supply situations, the paper house would warehouse its needs to ensure paper availability; in slack times, it might have shipments made direct from factory at cost savings. Constant communication of changes enabled the supplier to adjust his own plans. When an accident made necessary rerunning of a large mailing, the supplier made a successful effort to secure a duplicate paper order in a tight market situation.

By communication which considered the agency's paper supply needs as a mutual problem and enlisting the supplier in working for a mutual objective, the agency management created a relationship which was beneficial and satisfying to both.

Similar approaches apply to relationships with other community agencies. All have community betterment as a common objective. Dialogue discloses common problems and exchange of information on handling them is of benefit to all. Where two agencies provide identical services, relationships may be improved by each one's concentrating on different areas or age groups. Or, it may be discovered that the need is great enough for two and that a common promotional effort can increase response and shave per capita costs.

Relations with individuals, such as volunteers, members, program participants and users of services are based on common goals. But in these continuing dialogue is essential. Good relations may be marred by failure to look and listen for complaints. Once a program is rolling along and seems to be going well, don't assume this will continue. Failures of physical things or of people can damage relations and destroy enthusiasms. A class teacher develops a mental problem and neglects teaching. A steam radiator creates noise interference. Shower room outlets provide no hot water. If neglected, some people will complain—but others will just drop out.

Where supervisory personnel are too few to monitor all such problems, other means for maintaining dialogue can be arranged. One client in a group can be delegated to report periodically how things are going and advise promptly of an emergency situation. An advisory group with representatives from each constituency may be set up. Sometimes a scholarship participant can be assigned responsibility for reporting that index of success or failure—attendance—and for advising of any causes for complaint.

Determining One's Publics

Among public relations professionals, every group important to an organization's success and with whom it needs to maintain continuing communication is called a "public." Besides the internal groups, many segments of the general public have common interests which make communication with them as groups advisable. There are the community leaders—city, state or other government officials, boards of civic improvement associations, clergy associations, service clubs, women's club leaders, media personnel.

In general, these publics are of opinion-makers, the persons who are interested and active in trying to improve a community and whose collective evaluation of your organization determine its image as publicly perceived.

While a United Way committee evaluates an organization on its report of services rendered and to be rendered, people in these publics are more likely to judge it by its representatives who appear in public, who serve on committees and councils, or who speak before their group meetings.

Relations Are Everyone's Responsibility

Communication for developing good relationships is too large a task to be handled alone by official spokespersons and public relations directors. Even the receiving clerk at the trucking platform has responsibility—for maintaining good relations with the suppliers' drivers. Their goodwill may mean a great deal to you in getting an emergency shipment to you as fast as possible.

Institutions which neglect to communicate to their employees the need for building good public relations have overlooked those who already have a vested interest in the organization's success. Their dependence upon a paycheck should give them a proprietary feeling which can be enlisted in the agency's service.

Where this feeling is lacking, it often arises from poor internal communication or lack of it. Such comments as "Nobody cares" or "Nobody tells me anything" are symptoms of communication neglect. The feed-the-starving-Chinese but neglect-the-children-at-home syndrome is evident in too many communication programs. It often affects agencies preoccupied with problems of the larger community.

Yet one eminent public relations professional notes that no institution has yet been known to maintain good relations with its community while neglecting internal relations. Employees are supposedly insiders and with people outside the organization their comments and attitudes can carry great weight.

Staff members and employees need to know they are part of the communication team—that their comments affect the agency's image and its acceptance and support by others. A camp leader needs to realize that his/her salary may be affected by relationships with parents. Whether a father says, "Look what they did **for** my kid!" or "Look what they did **to** my kid!" may determine his contribution and that of his friends as well.

However unjustified, a father's complaint needs to receive a staff member's sympathetic hearing before he/she describes the circumstances which led to an upsetting occurrence.

To make good communicators among employees, one should talk and write about specifics—programs, activities, achievements, goals. Employees understand and relate to these and can in turn talk to others about them. It is the broad brush statements and generalities, however idealistic and philosophically commendable, that lead to unachievable hopes and disappointed expectations, to anger and frustration. Better also to be modest in claims and in implied promises than to lay a base for future bitterness.

A workshop on internal communication arrived at this consensus among professionals for four guidelines to communication with employees:

Authenticity—participation by top management to give authority.

Mutuality—communicating to employees in terms of their own interests and in a framework of dialogue.

Continuity—so that communication becomes a relationship, not an emergency measure after neglect.

Credibility—integrity of statement in line with organizational performance and timed relative to a good climate for communication.

However logical it may have appeared to those in charge of policy-making and the treasuror, an announcement of a groundbreaking ceremony for a new building did not sit well with employees whose requests for wage increases had just been rejected for lack of funds. Employee relations were badly hurt.

Yet, through continuing communication, employees can come to share their leaders' dream of better working quarters and rejoice in the sizeable gift which makes it possible. They can be made to realize that a building is a long-term separate matter from the drive for increased memberships which fell short of its goal and resulted in inadequate funds for across-the-board raises.

Good member relations is aided by continual, consistent and clear communication about official rules and regulations. It is not enough to advise members they must take a shower before entering the swimming pool. One must explain the need to avoid contamination. One must post reminder signs near the entrance. One must get members to help with the enforcement by reminding delinquent ones for their own protection. Here are examples:

Enforcing the Rules--
Three Case Histories

No one, even in the military, can issue an order with assurance it will be carried out. It is doubly true in today's permissive society and in volunteer organizations. Feedback is essential to assure that a message is received, understood correctly and acted upon. Beyond this, management must monitor performance and reissue instructions where needed.

A central city youth-and-adult organization executive finds this difficult to impress on its younger professional staff. Too often, he finds, they are ill-equipped with mastery of words, grammar and syntax to write easily and effectively. At the time he finds them reluctant to confront youngsters using the gymnasium, for instance, with violation of the rules.

After members of the athletics staff have labored at the typewriter to produce a memorandum, or struggled to design and post a sign, they appear to feel that their responsibilities for rules enforcement have ended. Although sneakers are required for shooting baskets on the basketball court, they will walk past fully-clothed youngsters in shoes so engaged without even calling the infraction to their attention. He has struggled to change these staff members' attitudes with mixed success and failure.

In a different community a similar organization mailed rules for use of the swimming pool to all members. These required caps for girls and boys with long hair, soap suds shower before entering the pool, swimming in assigned lanes, drying off before entering the locker room after swimming, among other things. A posted sign by the locker room door reiterated the drying-off rule. Yet many of the swimmers continued to ignore this or other regulations.

Communication had begun to break down when non-members were admitted for one-day or one-week swimming during the summer season without ever receiving a copy of the rules. The aquatics director was at camp and others carried out supervision. Also, new members were not acquainted with the rules until mailed copies after their applications were processed at the main office; meanwhile they were using the pool. Verbal reinforcement of the rules was not given by the clerk who received the pool fees nor by the lifeguards in charge. Training and instructions to the lifeguards did not impress upon them the reasons for the rules and their importance. Nor did they receive instructions on how to handle infractions. Spreading disregard for the rules caused resentment in conscientious members and general lack of observance.

By contrast, another community institution with a pool had no noticeable difficulty with observance. Each new group of swimmers were conducted through locker rooms and other facilities at which time the rules and reasons for them were explained. Opportunities for questions were offered at each step. Instructions in conduct and courtesy stressed consideration for others. Safety and health matters were discussed. Only when each person had been given a copy of the rules and said he or she understood them was a pool admission card issued.

If rules are important, an agency will convey that idea to its members and constituents by the detail of its communication and by its attitude toward them as expressed in the effort it makes to enforce them. The last agency described does not take lightly damage to its equipment, and as a result, has had comparatively little expense for such repairs which have run high in some institutions.

Sometimes trying to get a communication through channels is similar to lacing a pair of boots with shoe string which has lost its metal tips, as the following illustrates.

Avoiding Distortion of the Message

Face to face methods of communication are not always the most effective when channeled through several persons. The message tends to lose something in translation. It may become necessary to bypass established lines in order to make certain program leaders carry out a central organization's intention.

This is what one area Girl Scout Council learned. The councils' decision about a positive step in interracial relations was not "getting through" to the 3,000 active volunteer leaders of local units as intended. The channels of communication were: central administrators to local boards, to troop leaders, to individual scouts. The program was not being implemented where it counted. Something must be done.

To make certain all leaders received the message in the same form, the first step was to put out a regional mailing to the 3,000, followed by a once-a-month newspaper report of progress. The council created a task force with representation from each local unit to receive training in awareness of interracial differences and problems.

At the training sessions, instructors pointed out the differences in people's backgrounds and their exposure to concepts and information that resulted in their feeling differently about many things. The instructors showed how obstacles to communication arise from the girls' own natural inclination to stay with their friends, splitting into two camps of integrated nature. They explained how attempts to communicate between races may be frustrated by preconceptions and stereotyping—for example, the notion that all whites come from privileged backgrounds and other ethnic groups from underprivileged families.

In the course of training, the representative leaders and staff members were called upon to play roles in resolving conflicts. They were shown how to bring resentments out into the open quickly before they became explosive—such as some campers' anger toward those who failed to carry their fair share of the work load. Leaders were especially instructed to be sensitive to the real but hidden meaning of remarks and actions and to bring out the reasons for them through objective questioning.

Need for this surfaced when one leader misinterpreted as unpatriotic the remark of a black girl that she wished she lived in Africa. The leader saw this as a lack of appreciation of the advantages of living in the United States. By remaining open and inquiring why the girl felt this way, she might have found out that, quite the contrary, the black girl greatly sympathized with the less fortunate people whom circumstance had placed on the continent of her ancestors. On reflection, she appeared motivated by impulses similar to those of white girls of an earlier generation who volunteered for missionary service in Africa.

Eventually, the Girl Scout organization decided to extend its program to the earliest ages in scouting: the Brownie packs of 7- and 8-year olds of second and third grade school levels. It adopted the Green Circle program, developed by Quakers, which helps a youngster understand her growing awareness of a wider and wider world around her—from parents, at first, to brothers and sisters, to friends, to acquaintances, to strangers.

Experiencing how it seemed to be inside or outside a circle, the youngsters also were helped to understand people's feelings about symbols, such as the Cross, Star and Crescent, about the nature of green things and their capacity for growth. They were taught to apply the lessons learned to people outside their own circle of friends. Programs can communicate.

In the case of the original communication about positive interracial approaches which failed, the scout leaders finally achieved success by using several techniques. When they discovered the message was distorted in transmission by the official communication channels, they used written communication to avoid alteration and weakening of its impact. Next, they found the climate was not favorable for action because troop leaders' lack of experience and knowledge of minority attitudes and feelings made them ill-equipped for the task. The sensitivity training and role playing used in training task force members overcame this and enabled the representative leaders to educate others also. In the Green Circle programs the Girl Scout Council was essentially applying this effective communication technique to its youngest charges. Publicizing case histories of improvements in race relations enforced the message, enabling the troop leaders to see that the program worked, and motivated each to want to do as well.

Communication objectives of improving relations with ethnic groups and their friends were achieved by this communication effort. It also contributed to an image of the Girl Scout organization as an innovative leader in resolving interpersonal and intergroup problems.

Sharing Objectives vs. Negotiation

Organizations build images with solid achievements and communication of those achievements to enhance their reputations. They build relationships by awareness and sharing—or by negotiations.

In neither case do institutions need to give up their own identities or distinctive points of view. But which direction they take in any relationship makes a difference in the communication goals and methods. Each party in a relationship must feel that it is advantageous to it for the relationship to be enduring. In the environment of sharing, communication is open and free; in negotiation, the environment is somewhat difficult. The groups are not necessarily adversaries, but both may be suspicious of the other's motives or reliability and, like a poker player, feel they must disclose their resources, strategy, or true intentions carefully and on a quid pro quo basis.

Churches and synagogues band together in community religious associations. Without giving up any denominational customs or beliefs, they find they have a great deal in common. They can work together for a better community on specific projects like chaplain services for hospitals and prisons, regulation of alcoholic beverage sales, senior citizens and youth center projects. Communication on these matters can be open; agreement on shared objectives comes easily. An ecumenical spirit of good will leads to enthusiasm and a common announcement of shared positions in resolutions which are published in newspapers and transmitted by their representatives appearing before government bodies. These can gain editorial and community leadership support and action by the power structure. A common objective of all religious bodies is realized by a sharing and uniting of effort to effectively communicate their concern for a problem and their agreement on a solution.

On other matters, however, no common ground may be found. Of such are the proposal for an abortion clinic in town, an agitation for Sunday business closings, and a suggestion to get smoking in the high school out of the men's and women's rooms by establishing rooms for smoking. Here dialogue reveals that consciences are divided, that practical considerations intervene. Any goal for religious association communication must be arrived at by negotiation.

Lines of opposition are drawn between right-to-life advocates who look upon abortion as murder, and women's rights supporters who see a female's right to control her body as paramount. In between are those who would undo the work of rapists, who feel medical judgments should prevail, or who view population control as the all-important issue if humanity is to survive. Pro-abortionists may believe the most important consideration is to avoid revival of black market abortions with their dangers to life and health of young girls. Perhaps all can come to unity through negotiation on an objective of preventing an abortion clinic in a specific neighborhood—because of the kind of traffic it will attract to the area and the encouragement of sexual license it will give through its high visibility. Each side gives up some of its goals in the interest of obtaining agreement on a specific project.

As between Sunday observers and Seventh Day observers, there may seem to be no agreement possible. Both may want a day of relative quiet free from commercial activities. Convictions about which day is to be considered holy are too deeply held to permit either to convince the other. Yet if both feel strongly enough, could they perhaps agree on two days of "rest"? At this point practical considerations intervene.

Saturdays and Sundays when most people are off work prove to be the biggest shopping days for many stores. Can they compromise on a less commercial atmosphere by licensing establishments to operate six days per week with a choice of Saturday or Sunday? Can certain areas be closed for one day or the other? By delving for the others' deeper concerns, it may be shown that Seventh Day advocates are interested primarily in one area, Sunday advocates in others. By conceding something each side may gain something else and arrive at a program which, while failing to accomplish all their original objectives obtain their essential needs.

Smoking rooms in the high school may suggest a different type of negotiation. Objective of the proponents is to get the smokers away from areas which must be frequented by nonsmokers and spare them the health hazards smoking creates. Opponents, on the other hand, may see this as a moral issue, giving a stamp of official approval by providing quarters for its practice. By negotiation, a program may be developed whereby the establishment of smoking rooms will be accompanied by lectures on the dangers of tobacco to health to be compulsory for all students. A rational approach to the problem may result in agreement where a moral approach may prove divisive.

In the first instance, negotiation succeeded through finding an overriding consideration which enabled both pro- and anti-abortion advocates to unite on a program. In the second instance, a **quid pro quo**—educational instruction on effects of smoking—sustained the principle which the objectors had found a roadblock to their joining in an agreement. But such bargaining strategies are no substitute for the two basics of successful negotiation:

Listening. In communication where the purpose is to agree upon mutual objectives and programs, listening is similar to that of a therapist in uncovering motivations and emotional hangups. One never takes words at face value. Some people do not know how to put their feelings into words; others may be unaware of their concealed desires behind the goals they say they are pursuing. One must listen for what the other fails to say, for clues to what considerations are really minor and which are paramount. Thoughtful listening, with attention to facial expressions and body language and what they imply, provide guidance about how agreement may be reached; what wording will satisfy opponents of a resolution, what aspect can be omitted to win support. If you are to get around an impasse, such listening should at first be without interruptions or objections but only with questions to give you a clearer understanding.

On a matter of Sunday closing, if you are an advocate, you will want to know a number of things about objectors' attitudes. Is their objection a matter of conscience—of deeply held conviction about Seventh Day observance? Or is it a practical consideration as they see a potential of losing one of their best business days in the week? Would they welcome closing on both Saturday and Sunday?

If you favor Sunday closing, you will want to know whether opponents are really only concerned about certain areas of the community which they serve. Perhaps a compromise can be reached on a basis of licensed establishments open six days weekly with a choice by the proprietor about whether to close Saturdays or Sundays.

Opponents, on the other hand, might try to discover whether those proposing Sunday closing really want to force others to accept their own convictions. Perhaps their motivation is only to achieve a day free of noise, traffic, congestion and other annoyances which interfere with rest, meditation and worship. Can this be achieved in some way agreeable to both types of advocates of Sabbath-day observance?

Mutual advantage. For any agreement to stand up it must include advantages for both sides which make them feel better off with it than without it. Traditionally, the Red Cross declined to join United Way drives because its leaders claimed it received more moneys by direct appeal than it would by sharing in the common effort. With its prestigious relation with the Federal Government, its easy access to media publicity—especially in times of disasters—and its long-standing image as a successful institution, it felt no need for joining others. The same has been true of several national organizations devoted to medical problems, notably those with a limited rather than broad-spectrum appeal.

In some instances, participation of such an organization may be vital to the success of a joint effort and special effort needed to reach agreement. Such concessions as granting rights for special appeals for disasters or inclusion of their literature in community mailings, with opportunity for contributors to designate contributions, may be needed to satisfy an organization that it will be more advantageous to cooperate.

Good relationships are built upon communication that honestly states one's own organization's purposes and points of view, but with a willingness to listen and to consider what others say —to modify one's own stand in the light of new evidence, in the interest of fairness, or to obtain a program by which everyone will benefit despite some sacrifice of minor goals.

CHAPTER XIV

COMMUNICATION TO BUILD MEMBERSHIP

To organizations which have an enthusiastic group of members, a prestigious image, limited facilities, and a waiting list of applicants, building membership may seem no problem. For others just keeping the membership roll from shrinking may be a major task. In a growing community, the principal objective may be to expand services and broaden the support base.

Whatever its situation, every organization should have a policy which delineates who its intended members are and how it proposes to serve them. The same applies to every program which may include non-members. From these will be derived goals—so many family memberships, so many singles, so many juniors, so many seniors. Goals will be set with maximum use of facilities in mind, relying on different hours of activities for working people, school children and senior citizens, for example.

Some organizations with an already enthusiastic membership group which wants more of the same may need only to let it be known that there are a few membership openings. There are no salespersons like members who want to share their good fortune with their friends. When expanding membership, it may be advisable to provide members with descriptive literature—or ask for lists of prospects to whom the organization can mail an invitation to join. You can have them address envelopes to their friends so that the handwriting is recognizeable. But for those agencies with higher goals, an organized campaign is needed.

A membership drive calls for building a prospect list, planning a coordinated promotion effort, personal solicitation, follow-up, application acknowledgement, and introducing the new member to the organization.

Building a List of Prospects

Present members are usually a good source of member prospects. Even when members refuse to solicit memberships personally, they will often be happy to supply names of people they would like to have invited to join. In addition, there are classified lists which can be borrowed, purchased or rented.

Depending on types of members you are seeking, consider school lists, community residence directories, association membership lists. Commercial organizations maintain up-to-date mailing lists of many types and will sometimes rent a portion for a single geographic area in which you are interested. If you would like to increase your membership among professional people, for example, directories of dental and medical society members are readily available. Classified telephone books are keys to commercial people or reference directories may be found in the public library.

Where a professional association or union, for example, may be unwilling to release its membership list for such a mailing, it may approve your program and offer to inform its membership by including your literature in a mailing of its own or to announce your drive in its own membership bulletin. Such an announcement constitutes an implied endorsement and may be more valuable than your own mailing.

Some organizations build lists of prospects by announcing their program in newspapers or broadcasts by publicity or advertising. To obtain the largest response, it is usually desirable to offer more information by calling a phone number or writing to someone at an announced address. If your announcement is perceived by the media as performing a genuine public service, they may be generous with print space or air time in order to assist you.

Publicity can reveal a whole new area of prospects, but should not be counted upon to sell any organization or program. Name, address and telephone number of everyone expressing interest in response to publicity, advertising or other promotional effort should be entered on a prospect card and filed for later follow-up. Any comments pertinent to future solicitation should be noted, such as a specific activity in which the prospect shows interest. All cards should be dated so that you can later tell whether a prospect is likely to be a "live" one.

Most important in building prospects is not to require people to commit themselves to very much by their first response. To ask a stranger to send check for full membership fee with application as a first contact may well lead to their failure to respond at all. The point of all successful promotions is to make response as effortless and inviting as possible.

Planning Membership Promotion Program

As an example of membership building, let's suppose you are organizing a suburban executive health club. Limited facilities and space dictate that it be restricted to men. Most likely prospects would appear to be members of management within a 4-mile radius who could come for workouts during the noon hour. Other good ones might be commuters who would use the facility during evening hours.

Local companies having an interest in keeping their executives healthy might be willing to release management lists for your mailing—or better still, to circulate your announcements internally with a word of approval. If you are able to sell company presidents sufficiently, some may be glad to underwrite the program for a key management group.

You can obtain a list of such companies from your local chamber of commerce, perhaps with names of presidents and personnel vice presidents. You can get more company names from the classified section of the telephone directory and call their operators for officials' names.

Clergymen, as well as businessmen, may be both prospects and sources for identifying those neighboring executives who work out of town. The local religious association can supply a clergy list.

Your plan for membership promotion may include the following:

1. Briefing for board and staff so they can answer questions of others; staff instructed on how to handle inquiries and applications.

2. Letter to presidents and/or personnel vice presidents of local companies: stress importance of executive health, including statistics on losses annually to business due to absences for illnesses or under-performance by executives not in top condition. Describe your proposed plan briefly with offer of further information.

3. Telephone follow-ups requesting approval. Explore ave-

nues of information leading to their executives. Inquire about their experience with executives suffering heart attacks, ulcers, alcoholism and the like. This may motivate them and provide you with further evidence for selling others. Ask for their lists of executives and whether they would be willing themselves to forward your literature to all executive personnel.

4. Plan an open house for all prospects and their wives so they can inspect the facilities. Decorate club with posters on dangers to which executives are exposed and statistics on how fitness programs enable them to cope with business stresses. Provide demonstrations. Have staff available to answer questions, conduct tours, and accept applications.

If groups promise to be sizeable, extend open house over several evenings. Send tickets with specific dates along with letters of invitation. Address invitations to home and to husband and wife. Inclusion of the wives is particularly important because they may be more concerned about the husband's health than is the executive himself. Also, if the husband is to take off another night during the week, for example, the wife may oppose it unless she understands and approves the reason.

5. Prepare a register or cards for guests to sign when they enter so that you have a record of attendees for the prospect list. Ask for name, address and telephone number. If cards are collected as people leave, ask for comments. One way to assure getting names of those reluctant to fill out cards is to prepare name badges for all guests and serve light refreshments. Encouraging social conversation can be used to get acquainted with prospects and to make further points about the need for participation in fitness programs.

6. Release advance publicity to local media—newspapers, radio, television, company employee publications. Prepare a series of articles on executive health for each medium; offer director of health club as subject for broadcast and newspaper interviews on subject. Encourage director to cite specific cases from his/her experiences in previous clubs, and of disasters to companies from key executive heart attacks; also, company reduction of losses from ill health through fitness programs; and the like.

7. Mail follow-up material to all prospects with details of specific services: hours for programs, for fitness evaluations, for individual program consultations. Include application forms. Offer company-wide services.

8. Place advertising in business publications and business page of newspapers.

9. Appoint staff member to handle membership program records with responsibility for keeping card files on prospects and members, and how expression of interest in each case originated (phone call following company mailing, publicity, visitation at open house, etc.). This information is helpful in future promotion to show what methods proved most effective. File cards should also indicate individual's specific interests (swimming, jogging, exercise machines) and any indication of intention to join. Staff member should be trained to nail down appointments for physical fitness analysis sessions and program recommendations; also, any known physical problems and doctor's approval where needed.

10. Assign person for telephone follow-ups when scheduling deadlines approach and for mailing out confirmations of appointments and receipts.

As the above plan is put into operation, it will be necessary to assign time segments for achieving numbers of members and for constant monitoring to determine whether goals are being met. If efforts at enrolling commuter members lags, for example, one might print flyers to be passed out in railroad stations and posted on bulletin boards and in buses where commuters will observe them. Perhaps those commuters already enrolled might be enlisted to pass along handbills to their fellow commuters.

Resourcefulness is an essential quality in any communication specialist, along with alertness to developments which call for innovative approaches. By use of creative imagination, some agency communication professionals are able to achieve cost-savings and short cuts. This quality is also necessary where a changing environment leads to failure of once tried-and-true methods.

Responding to Feedback

Alert organizations provide a way for listening to and responding to prospect and member comments or complaints. Ofttimes these provide the key to greater success in member promotion. These may even lead to revisions of programming and planning as it is realized that the constituencies are changing or that their needs have changed.

One inner-city church's diminishing membership presented a dilemma. All standard efforts to reverse a trend failed. Analysis showed that company transfers, deaths of older members and moves to retirement communities were draining away members faster than new ones could be found. Newcomers to the community were from a motley of ethnic and national groups replacing what had been primarily a middle-and upper-income white population.

The church had always been an activist organization, sponsoring sports teams and youth organizations, supporting home and foreign missionary efforts, entertaining returning missionaries and exchange students, sponsoring refugee families and foreign clergy education in this country. As a result, its membership was a cosmopolitan mixture of races and nationals along with its traditional base. The former group was growing.

With its white senior citizens and its younger multi-ethnic families, the church began to respond to needs by instituting Meals-on-Wheels for elderly shut-ins, a day care nursery for working mothers, groups for singles, married couples, parents without partners. It used drama, dance, and a variety of music —classical, ethnic, gospel and jazz—in its services to appeal to wide-ranging cultural backgrounds. Still the downward trend in members gradually continued. Publicity and promotion of innovations brought visitors, but not enough members among the people of contrasting cultures and religious convictions.

As the ecumenical movement opened up cooperation among competing religious bodies, the church freely offered its facilities for community activities and one of these was a weekly "Learning for Living" program sponsored by the local religious association, especially for senior citizens. The city had built a number of apartment houses for retirees; others began to move into the area when a senior citizens center was instituted. After several years of operation, the "Learning for Living" program has now become "sold out" on opening day.

This program introduced the many older persons to the church's ample and lovely facilities, led to many becoming members. The friendly atmosphere has kept them coming back and brought the member drain to a standstill.

Overcoming its difficulty of communicating with the Hispanic people moving into the area, the church instituted a Sunday school class in Spanish which promises to bring further growth to the church. Each of these activities was instituted in response to an observed need—and most of them resulted from feedback (member and prospect comments) which led to perception of a need.

Making the Program the Communication Medium

Newspaper stories may create interest without persuading people to join. For this you may need a persuader. Stores offer bargain days—something to get customers to take action rather than delaying. Social agencies can hold open house days, or guest nights when members bring friends and prospects for get-acquainted socializing. Awards nights are also a good time for inviting prospects who can join in honoring the achievers while, perhaps, acquiring a desire to join in and become achievers themselves.

Getting people to see a program in action surpasses all other means for communicating what it is all about. On such occasions, it is well to have guides to explain it and answer questions. Sometimes the performers, as at a craft fair, are themselves the best ones to explain what the action is all about. Outdoor field day competitions and festivals may call for announcers with loudspeakers to describe the activities for all guests.

Diversity of programs and services may be considered communication handicaps, requiring many and various promotion activities. One 4-H Club Association has simplified this confusing task by turning the diversity into an asset. Its programs result from the expressed desires of the members, and most of them are led by enthusiastic volunteer leaders. Therefore the association stages an annual fair in which every group participates.

At the 4-H Fair, each group is responsible for a booth in which it demonstrates or exhibits its activities, with members present to recruit new participants. Activities range from such traditional ones as bread baking to rocketry and radio-controlled model airplanes. Quieter ones are stamp collecting and chess. But karate, motorcycle competitions and horsemanship also have a place in a larger arena.

For three days and nights, members of the 4-H Clubs demonstrate and explain their hobbies for crowds totaling 50,000 over the entire period. Fifteen acres of a county park are made available for the occasion, with twenty additional acres devoted to automobile parking. Except for coordination by a small staff, the entire fair is staged by volunteers. Admission is free, the few large expenses (for tents and buses) being assumed by sponsors or covered by a 20% share of proceeds from benefit sales of refreshments by community service groups.

As a communication vehicle, the fair is effective. Its two-hour minimal tour provides the visitor with a survey of what one county 4-H organization is all about. 4-H membership has continued to soar.

Soliciting Memberships Personally

Personal cultivation of membership is most effective because of immediate feedback. Frank, open responses can show why individuals are, or are not, interested. They can point to what has gone wrong in communication and permit its prompt correction. It is necessary to train those seeking members to listen for, and report back, reasons for turn downs.

For example, members asked to invite friends and acquaintances may find that your schedule conflicts with that of some other popular program. Or you may learn that there is a misunderstanding about requirements for admission, or unawareness that fees can be paid by installment arrangement. Where a prospect likes the idea but hesitates, personal solicitors should probe for a reason, perhaps one the prospect is embarrassed to mention. Where reasons begin to form a pattern, you feel compelled to change your plans to remove the obstacle. For a YMCA's executive fitness program, this was lack of adequate parking nearby and led to provision for its own parking lot.

Maintaining membership is equally important to inviting new prospects. Members are presumably best prospects because they already have shown interest and are acquainted with the services you offer. While personal circumstances and interests change, a growing attrition of members calls for a careful look at the causes. It may mean that communication has broken down with members or that the agency management has been preoccupied otherwise and ignored complaints.

Sometimes paid personal solicitors are the answer to a membership problem.

Mystery of the Missing Members

One community service agency in a fast-growing area had a membership problem. Too many members were failing to renew when the year ended. Searching for a solution, the executive director asked a woman working part-time on a program to devote additional time to finding the answer.

Working from home for a modest fee, she contacted each lapsed member. Though it was often necessary to call them at odd hours or in person, she discovered the reason for the dropout in each case.

Her earliest reports disclosed a feeling among certain adult members that they were being neglected in the agency's programming. As a result the board voted to install a universal gymnasium. Later it added a paddle tennis court adjacent to the aquatics building. Hours were changed for some facilities. These decisions, plus the personal attention, were able to lower the rate of membership loss substantially.

As a result of this success, the management extended this membership cultivation program to include new prospects. The woman representative was directed to secure names and addresses of every new resident and to call upon each family personally. She explains in detail the facilities, services and programs which the agency provides for every age from preschoolers to senior citizens. She leaves literature detailing costs, hours, program objectives, and application forms. Before leaving the home, she notes the ages, sex, recreational and development needs of each family member, and offers to answer questions. As a final gesture of invitation she leaves a free guest pass entitling the family as a group to a one-time use of the swimming pool.

This method of introducing newcomers to the agency is credited with most of an annual membership gain of 15% in the first year of the program's operation.

The Indispensable Telephone

As a drive for membership nears its conclusion, the telephone becomes essential to reaching the objective by deadline. Season or course opening dates require a closing so that space and leadership can be assigned, facilities and equipment prepared, schedules revised if necessary. There may even be a need to cancel a program if enough members are not enrolled. If monitoring shows capacity has been reached, applications must sometimes be closed early.

In any case, the telephone becomes the medium by which late applicants can be notified and their disappointment be assuaged; or by which wavering prospects can be persuaded and doubtful inquiries eliminated from consideration. Someone can call all prospects reminding them of their expressed interest and advising that no further applications can be accepted after a certain date. Each card should be marked with indication of whether to eliminate the prospect from consideration or to keep on file for next year.

Acknowledging the Application

Building membership requires attention to communication with members from the time they apply. Each applicant should receive a prompt acknowledgement with a receipt for any fee enclosed. If an application must be processed, the member is entitled to know this and how soon he or she may expect to receive a membership card and be admitted to membership privileges. The card itself might well be accompanied by a form letter from the chairman of the board welcoming him/her to the organization and listing all the advantages membership brings.

In acknowledging memberships in specific programs only, an opportunity is presented to suggest the wider advantages of full membership. Without exerting any pressure which might be resented, an invitation is extended for future consideration.

Introducing the New Member

Long-standing members can become cliquish without intending to do so. They have formed friendships which they enjoy, sometimes to the point of ignoring newcomers. Organizations which want to grow find it desirable to make members communicators. Extroverts among them will enjoy welcoming the new members and introducing them around if passed a word of encouragement. Name badges for members, old and new, provide one method of getting acquainted. Where resistance is found, an agency can provide such badges as admission tickets to a program, indicating fee has been paid.

Keeping Membership Communication Open

An agency which provides for continuing communication to and from members should not have to employ a personal caller to find out why members drop out.

Although program directors may be well-trained to listen, report and act upon member suggestions and complaints, an indication of central management concern for members' views is also in order. If normal channels of communication do not bring a fair proportion of comments, a manager should consider whether this indicates perfect performance—or whether perhaps deeper probing is needed.

Several methods are available, such as: A questionnaire inviting comments with the annual bill for membership renewal; making a point of personally inquiring from a sample of membership.

Most important is that members' complaints lead to results or that they be informed why not. After a repetition of complaints about the lack of hot water in the showers, members may give up complaining as fruitless and look elsewhere for better service.

Some organizations have found that a complaint form for registering every member suggestion is desirable, with instructions to staff member receiving the complaint to send the original to the person responsible for action and a carbon copy to the executive director.

CHAPTER XV

PROMOTING A PROGRAM

Programs, like membership, require communication that moves to action called promotion. People who should be interested must be informed, urged to participate and given a reason to act promptly.

Before planning promotion one must find the answers to such questions as: What is the purpose of this program? What benefits does it offer to those who participate? Is there also a benefit to the community? What facts have we to support the claimed benefits? What aspects will most appeal to prospective members?

Who are the prospects? Where are they located? By what means can we communicate with them? When is the best timing for communication? If they represent separate groups, have we special appeals which should be considered for each?

What is the optimum goal for numbers of participants? With our prospects and the climate for communication existing, is it a reasonable and attainable goal? Have we the resources essential for successful promotion? What will be needed in the way of staff involvement? Of finances? What sort of scheduling and priority must be assigned to assure reaching the goal?

Sell the Purpose

Most important for any program is to establish, in the minds of prospects and other people who may be expected to recommend and support the program, what it will accomplish for participants and for the wider community. Let's say you are promoting a summer camp for girls. It is not enough to indicate that you provide a way for parents to get their children out of the home during the months the schools are closed.

If your camp is a sports camp, you must be prepared to show

that you offer tennis, golf, horseback riding and other activities which young people enjoy; that you have instructors who know the sports and can advance their students' skill. This reassures the parents their children's valuable summer months will be put to good use.

Whatever your camp stands for—character-building, aquatics, nature lore, crafts, educational advancement, music, exploring, travel, ecology awareness, historical restoration, or archeology—it is not enough to state this. Parents want to know why this is important to their youngsters. They need solid evidence that this is more than someone's dream. They need to know the credentials of the personnel and any record of performance to date, as well as the content of instruction to support the theme.

Another important point will be to indicate the levels of competition or instruction in each program. If you have a sports camp, a girl who is already advanced in tennis will want to know whether your instructor can take her to competence beyond her present ability and whether she will find there opponents who will challenge her best efforts. If you have programs for all aquatics skill levels, so that a girl can progress from beginner to advanced swimming and diving, this will be important to many young women.

Scout leaders have over the years established a reputation for camps which provide the outdoor life as a builder of self-confidence and competence. This, and the moral and ethical content of the program, are widely known although some more recently developed programs may require more explanation.

But a church sponsoring a religious and character-building camp will need to spell out its purposes in more detail. Will the youth merely meet for worship and instruction? Or will they be confronted with the challenges of contemporary society and helped to learn how to handle dilemmas they will face in school, work and family with concern and self-respect?

Select the Targets

With your purpose clearly in mind, next step is to decide who and where are the girls who should want to attend. Camps serving one geographical community are likely to be broader in appeal and more diverse in programs to serve a cross section. Specialized camps, such as those concentrating on sports or music, will need to reach a regional or even a national constituency to enroll the prospects they seek. They will use specialized media. For your typical camp prospects will probably be a dozen or score of communities within easy traveling range. Full use of the facilities may accommodate 400 girls, let's say. You set that as your goal.

Of course, if you have split sessions you might double that. Or, you might set goals of 200 for entire summer registrations and 200 additional single session registrations for each camp period. These goals may need to be revised as the promotion campaign proceeds and applications indicate a tendency one way or the other. Depending on the kind of program you offer, you may want to give priority to those who will remain longer and therefore benefit more—or stress exposure of more girls to the instruction by emphasizing short-term participation.

In order to enroll 400, you will need a large prospect list. If experience has shown that you will have 8 per cent return, let's say, and 5 per cent registration, you will want 8,000 names. That appears to be a large list to compile from the small city and 14 towns you serve. You calculate the costs of assembling these lists, of folders, letters and postage for getting your message to them. There must be a more efficient way of communicating! There is.

You have an advantage over national camps. Your people are within easy driving distance. You can assemble them to talk to them in groups, or send representatives to them. You decide to reach them in groups. You will have one big meeting in central city with a broadcast invitation, but in each small community and in city neighborhoods you will arrange meetings in homes at which staff members will present your camp story.

Primary targets will be experienced campers and their friends. Girls who have attended previously can talk knowingly about your camp and convey their enthusiasm to others. If new prospects already know someone who has attended, the information they receive is more convincing than from a stranger.

Put a Plan Together

Organizations which use camp as a builder of full memberships, and members as prospects for camp, have one advantage: Their camp promotion is a continuing process as each feeds the other. They can have a camp publication daily or weekly during the summer season and monthly or quarterly during the rest of the year. With chatty news about councilors and campers, their school achievements, birthdays, newest interests, a mimeograph or printed newsletter can maintain much of the family-type relationships and interest in each other which makes them eagerly anticipate next season's get-together.

Mailed at second or third class rates, such a publication can carry your promotion messages less expensively in form of news. There will be stories on new courses and programs, new staff members, new facilities, advance registrations, and the like which sharpen interest in attending.

But your girls camp serves a number of communities, and you have no branches with winter season programs in many communities. So the membership building trade-off applies chiefly to your central city. Perhaps a quarterly publication for the camp will still be advantageous.

So you jot down a promotion plan with target dates and reminders of details not to overlook. It might look something like this:

CAMP PROMOTION

September   Get councilors and campers who worked on newspaper to write memories of summer sessions
-- Anecdotes, amusing incidents, inspiring moments, worthwhile experiences.
-- Ask for snapshots as illustrations where available.
Get lists of award winners, achievement certificates, competition results.
Review official photos of camp season.
-- Sort for subject matter, related story-telling action shots.
--Decide whether drawing will be needed to illustrate any point for which photo is unavailable.

October   Assemble and edit material received for autumn issue of camp newsletter.
Include appeal for additional comments and photos for future issue.
Ask for names of friends who would be interested in

receiving future issues.
Assign responsibility for mailing list and direct person in charge how to handle it.
Mail issue.

November Canvass parents of campers for usable comments on what camp did for their daughters.
Make plans for early spring rally of campers in central city—a reunion of old-timers with all councilors available present, along with invited friends and prospects: also parents.
Jot down ideas for slide talks.

December Review responses to fall newsletter and plan winter issue.
Review all photos for multiple uses and order duplicates where same photo may be used in newsletter, slide talk, promotion folder, publicity releases, etc.

January Edit winter issue and plan production.
Lay out photo spread, write captions.
Edit letters, reports of camp memories.
Write copy for rounded issue, including early plans for next season.
Announce date of camp reunion rally with names of councilors and staff expected to be present, also pictures where possible.
Canvass availability of camp personnel to lead follow-up rallies in other communities, slide presentations in campers' homes.

February Mail winter issue of newsletter.
Send form letter to mothers of previous campers with query about willingness to hold afternoon tea or evening get-together for camper and friends who are prospects some time in spring at which slide talk can be presented and questions answered.
Collect in one file folder every fact needed for preparation of promotion materials: names and descriptions of camp programs, courses and activities; councilors, leaders and staff—their training and certification in area of responsibility, previous experience and third person testimony; facilities; food,

safety and health; opportunities for individual camper development; stories and achievements of camping in previous years for illustrating your points; location of camp with map and/or other instructions for getting there; requirements for admission including any doctor's or other immunization certificate; dates of sessions; clothes or other personal articles required. Write each kind of item on separate card for easy organization later.

Get out the pictures from previous camp sessions including snapshots submitted by campers and councilors. Place a card with idea to be illustrated on top of each subject pile: food, crafts, health and safety, etc. Evaluate them for (1) print quality and (2) communication adequacy. As you work on this project from year to year, you learn to plan a year ahead for photos you need to be taken during camp sessions.

Prepare a basic document encompassing all pertinent information which cannot be left to question-and-answer periods or other inquiries. From this you will later draw information, sentences, paragraphs in preparing talks, folders, releases and other promotional communications.

Choose pictures and write copy for folder; order from printer, together with reply cards, envelopes or other inclosures, indicating meeting and mailing deadlines.

Lay out photographs to be used in slide talks in order of presentation; write split video-audio script for presentation, numbering pictures to be used in order keyed to script. Order slides.

March — Prepare newspaper releases with dates of release for reunion rally, camp opening advance story, camp opening, etc.

Rehearse slide talk with one or two friendly critics to spot the weak points. If projectionist rather than speaker-control operation is to be used, rehearse with projectionist. Check meeting arrangements. Check on printer that folders and registration blanks will be ready for central city rally.

	Send out release, and hold rally.
April	Check meeting dates for teas for campers and guests in home. Telephone follow-ups may be necessary. If others will give the slide talks instruct and rehearse them. In some cases slides and script may be provided to an uninstructed speaker, but the person must be knowledgeable enough to answer whatever questions may arise. Begin mailings to all prospects, and organize to handle mail and telephone inquiries. Monitor response volume on a weekly basis after mailings begin. Plan for telephone follow-up if needed.
May	Continue teas and follow-ups. Review registration volume to determine whether 400 target likely to be reached. Edit and publish spring issue of newsletter with reports on early registrations and late changes in schedule, personnel or programs. Inform board and all others concerned of progress. Send out advance release on camp season.
June	Prepare for publishing weekly camp newsletter. Send first-session editions to second-session registrations.

Hints on Executing Promotion Plan

Promotional communication has one advantage over many other forms: Feedback is in measurable form. An objective takes the form of so many inquiries, so many registrations, so much money. This contrasts with the vagueness of goals such as conveying information or changing people's attitudes. There is satisfaction in knowing just what has been accomplished—in being able to monitor continuously and adjust the promotional program accordingly when results are different than expected.

This is particularly true of a slide talk which will be given again and again. If response is less than enthusiastic, you can examine your content to see whether you have overlooked fundamentals.

Did you consider your audience? If you are talking to the

parents, did you include emphasis on health and safety—the training of your cook, the nutritious diet planning, the competence of the camp nurse, the availability of doctor and hospital in case of illness, the waterfront safety precautions and credentials of the aquatics director? Have you mentioned the competence and training of the bus drivers who transport the youngsters to and from camp?

If yours is a boys camp, have you emphasized things important to fathers, as well as mothers? Have you helped them understand how camp helps boys grow more mature under the direction of trained councilors? Have you included a few pictures of boys' accomplishments—a snapshot of the champion canoe racers or winner of the fishing contest holding up his catch and grinning ear to ear? The lure he made himself in close-up? You need many "hooks" like these for parents.

For the boys have you included enough "fun" things? Informal "horsing around" pictures? Interesting activities which don't appear like school work—competitions, story-telling around the campfire, building camp on an explorer expedition? Have you shown a picture of last year's group well-tanned and happy waiting for the bus that will take them home at the end of the season?

How about the presentation? Have you used speak-English— not the formal language of the classroom, but conversational language? When writing to be read aloud, write as you would talk normally—and when reading it, don't worry about the exact words. Speak as you feel—with interrupted sentences, offhand comments, and, when appropriate, humor.

Do you include enough anecdotes—camp incidents of last year which make your points seem more real? For example, do you have an illustration of a shy boy who returned from camp filled with self-confidence because in the wild life situation he had found his knowledge made him a leader?

If your mailings seem to generate many inquiries but not enough registrations, perhaps you have expected too much too soon? One way to find out is a telephone follow-up to see whether parents have some reservation which can be easily removed —some question they hesitated to ask at your rally. Did you fail to provide a telephone number to call or a person to write in your literature? Or has some situation caused them to lose interest? Perhaps they have merely failed to recognize the desirability of promptness. Did you advise them that the initial deposit is refundable up to a certain date—if they need to change their minds?

Checklist for Program Promotion

Chief difficulty in promotion is bringing all the parts together on time. In planning it is necessary to start with end product—the objective—and the final date for reaching it and plan backward with plenty of lead time to recoup in case of errors or delays. Here's a checklist of some trouble sources to avoid:

1. Have you allowed enough time for postoffice delivery of your mailing and of responses from prospects?

2. Do you have a firm commitment from printer for delivery of printing? Have you allowed additional leeway in case printer has unavoidable delay? Have you a contingency plan in case he does not deliver on time?

3. Have you given yourself more than enough time for preparation of copy for meeting printer's deadline—just in case you are interrupted by an emergency?

4. Has your copy indicated deadlines for orders or applications—or other reason for prompt action?

5. Have you lined up volunteers or blocked out staff time needed well in advance so that you are certain of support when you need it?

6. Have you prepared for recording all mail and phone inquiries by dates—both for monitoring and for next year's guidance—and for prospect list follow-up?

7. Have you trained people who will handle inquiries well in advance and blocked out your time for supervising their handling them in the beginning until their work becomes routine?

8. Have you provided flexibility for coping with peak loads when the difference between prompt processing of inquiries and delay may mean loss of registrants?

9. Have you cleared final drafts with everyone who has intimate knowledge of the program for last minute changes or oversights?

10. Has your plan for monitoring been set down on paper and charted with dates for intermediate decisions about follow-ups and alternate plans?

CHAPTER XVI

COMMUNICATING THROUGH THE ANNUAL REPORT

Accountability to supporters is important to any agency which hopes to keep and add to its clientele. While communication must be on a continuing basis, once annually the management expects to advise all financial sources how it spent every dollar contributed or paid for its services.

This should be looked upon not as an arduous task but as an opportunity to place a year's accomplishments in the framework of past history and of future challenges. You can present your stewardship in relation to the needs and the resources available. You can give your readers a feeling for the importance of your work and a satisfaction in having been a part of it.

Annual reports do require attention to details. But it is these details which give substance to claims of human service. When statistics are presented with pictures and case stories, this removes their dullness, and they come alive. Emphasis on clients who have been helped prevents an odor of puffery or of ego-building for leadership.

There is a place for recognizing and showing appreciation for those who have given dedicated service to the organization. But, with the exception of showing how volunteers have saved a need for money or extended the usefulness of contributed dollars, personal tributes can easily be overdone in annual reports. People read a report to find out what their dollars accomplished and what they can hope to accomplish by such contributions in the future.

Annual reports should be elaborate enough to communicate what agency supporters need to know, but not "fancy." A report which looks too expensive may well give a negative impression that money spent on the report might be used for services. Consider the case of the business corporation which sent out a slick paper annual report with pictures of the corporate officers and directors, factory buildings and products. It received a complaint from a "little old lady" stockholder who said, "Your fancy annual report must have cost at least one dollar. I'd rather have it in the dividend check."

Somewhere between the bare statement of financial summary and the "fancy" report is the happy mean which communicates the organization's performance and prospects in support of its purposes and image as defined by the board.

Make the Annual Report Communicate

Organizers of social institutions are motivated by a desire to solve problems and alleviate people's needs. Others contribute to their support because they perceive their purposes as worthy and their stewardship as conscientious. Annual reports, in financial statistics and interpretation of those statistics, need to support this image in terms of individual cases and of human concerns.

One way of doing this is with photographs. If the chairperson of the governing board (or other leadership figures) is shown, it should be in an action picture—perhaps conversing with a child or other client whom the organization serves. Show the program director and client with the architect examining model for the new health club. Show closeups of senior citizens or youth working in the craft shop.

Another way of humanizing reports is by printing case histories. More believability can be introduced with actual names, photos and case histories, both of clients and of volunteers who have helped with agency programs.

People like to read about the mother enabled to resume her work through the services of the child day care center or the accident victim enabled to again become self-supporting with a loan to buy a prosthesis. From such stories people gain an idea of how their gifts are put to work to help others and a feeling of satisfaction in having participated.

Of course, precaution must be taken to secure permission for such use of identifiable persons. Consideration for their sensitiveness and the law requires both asking permission and securing a written release. But when it is explained to them that in this way they can help others by encouraging further contributions, many will be glad to help. Anything which might be interpreted as pressure to give consent must be avoided. Otherwise, the person might feel exploited. Where there is potential for personal embarrassment, agency personnel should, of course, avoid any such use.

Interpreting Statistics

Statistical data in the raw are important to foundations, United Way, corporate contribution secretaries, government agencies and others who consider a variety of charities. With them, even more than with individual givers, you are competing with other causes and other institutions seeking similar ends. Where can they accomplish the most with the limited moneys at their disposal?

You can help them understand your figures by use of simple pie charts which show the sources of income on one hand and where it was used on the other. Such charts or bar charts can demonstrate the low portion of income spent on (1) fund raising and (2) overhead. These may vary from time to time, depending on such factors as concentration of expenses for a capital fund drive in one year and receipts from the drive in the following year. Where this happens, they must be clearly separated out and explained, using devices like dotted lines and captions.

One highly desirable chart series might show progress from year to year in coping with a problem. In an ongoing program such as swimming instruction, it could be very persuasive to show a dramatic growth from year to year in numbers of youngsters earning life-saving certificates. A statistic representing growth in case loads per staff member, on the other hand, might need some extensive explanation to indicate that quality of service is not sacrificed to quantity.

One chart which could greatly strengthen a report does not relate to dollars in direct terms. This is a chart of growth in volunteer services—both numbers of persons and hours spent. An agency with a strong program in enlisting and training volunteers might well feature this way of adding a multiplier and extending the effectiveness of every contributed dollar.

Budgeting future needs is also an important function of the annual report. You report to your supporters on the past and appeal for their continuing support by what you propose for the future. Bare figures are seldom sufficient. New opportunities for service arise; need for some older services may diminish, and they may be phased out. Record of solid performance in the past is usually a recommendation of equal potential for the future if your agency appears alert to change, not content to rest on a reputation already established. But new or extended programs must be sold by statistics which demonstrate need and a vision of what could be if your supporters will back you up.

Dispelling Groupwork Myths

Annual reports provide a vehicle for dispelling some myths about social agencies in general. Misconceptions grow up about every type of organization. Primarily, they come from generalizations from exceptional cases or from unconfirmed reports which are sensational and therefore widely circulated. Corrections seldom catch up with the original story.

Myth No. 1: Non-profit organizations are less efficient. Without a profit incentive, the impression goes, they tend to be less well-managed. Undoubtedly, there have been some agencies as ill-managed as some companies which have gone bankrupt. And in some cases, it may have taken longer for economic realities to catch up with them.

The annual report is a dynamic agency's opportunity. Management-by-objective enables chief executives to show what it will take to reach organizational goals in the year ahead, to monitor and tightly direct these activities so that, barring the unpredictable, they come out as planned. At year's end, it then becomes possible to show efficiency in terms of what was sought to be accomplished. It can often be asserted with assurance that the dedicated service of your people who have placed the needs of others above their own needs go beyond the call of duty. Their satisfaction comes from knowing their efforts are building a better community. Corresponding to "the bottom line" in business is the recognition of these achievements expressed by grateful supporters in the generosity of contributions.

Myth No. 2: Non-profit organizations are characterized by duplication and waste. This is the impression given the public at times when more than one institution offers the same service in a community. It is understandable that only so many persons can swim in a pool at the same time and therefore that a community needs more than a single pool. This is often not as readily perceived when there is duplication of a youth leadership training program or a senior citizens center. Competition, which is seen as healthy in business and in bringing out the best in both rivals, is sometimes viewed in community service as draining charitable contributions which might serve other needs.

Organizations need to justify such services, just as industrial corporations need to justify their product or service as providing something not otherwise available. In the case of senior centers, one may be in one end of town, the other in the other end. Older people may be unable to walk or manage transportation to a merged central city center. Youth training programs may appeal to different interests in young people. One may emphasize community service; another, political action; still others, sports or intellectual leadership. Annual reports can show the distinctive approach of such programs and the kinds of young people they help to develop leadership qualities.

Program distinction should be indicated whether geographical, cultural, ethnic or language group (e.g., Spanish-speaking), or age level. Generations often do not mix well: in music programs there is no reconciling lovers of classical music with those who prefer hard rock.

Myth No. 3. Professionals are less productive. This myth grows out of two facts. The output of assembly line workers who make a single product over and over is visibly measurable. How much a case worker accomplishes in the same time in listening to, and finding answers for, people with problems is harder to assess. In one case it may take a few minutes to come up with an answer—in another, it may take weeks.

Another source of the myth is the time it takes to create a program from an idea. When dealing with ideas, rather than tangible things, the chances for "goofing off" are seen to be greater. What is not so readily apparent is that the blue collar worker leaves his job at 4:30—or whenever his shift ends. The worker with ideas must live with them 24 hours a day until they are finalized.

Chief executives know how to keep the discussions on target and productive. Management-by-objective gives a C.E. an opportunity to insist that every staff member set his/her own targets for achievement and live up to the goals agreed upon. But quality of performance cannot always be conveyed in statistics. So there is an opportunity in the annual report to illustrate with a specific example or two of staff members' performance over and beyond the call of duty.

Reporting the Income Services

Agencies which receive program service fees from participants need to report these in some detail. Do fees pay for all out-of-pocket costs of a program? Do they contribute to, even support their share of overhead? Do they finance free scholarships for persons unable to pay?

Most agencies must be flexible enough to permit 15% of a program budget for free customers. Youth camp underprivleged youngsters may be included because of this flexibility. Do readers of your annual report understand their dollars are making this participation possible? When this is made clear, they may be much happier with partially self-sustaining programs.

Annual reports can be social documents which not only reinforce the public image of a single agency, but also uphold the value of privately-supported groupwork agencies generally. They can illustrate and emphasize these five distinct advantages such institutions offer: flexibility, volunteer services, people involvement, economy, and priorities which emphasize individual worth.

Because of the selfless devotion of people involved, "the bottom line" of such an institution's annual report is not expressed in dollars but in the development and growth of people—both volunteers and clients—the reduction of needs and dependency, and a steady improvement in the quality of life for its consumers of services and for the community. Its annual report should convey this.

CHAPTER XVII

KEEPING A LID ON COMMUNICATION COSTS

Communication activities in groupwork need cost analysis as much as the million dollar commercial advertising accounts. Control need not be as elaborate as those in advertising agencies, but attitudes and approaches may be similar.

Advertisers go to great lengths to consider the cost per hundred readers of a publication or of watchers of television. They analyze the nature of the audience of every communication medium they consider and decide whether a sufficient portion of that audience are potential customers for whatever they are selling. They time their advertising announcements seasonally to obtain greatest response and keep extensive records of direct inquiries and sales traceable to the advertisements—or of upturns in markets which specific media reach.

In the interest of making communication dollars go farther and accomplish more, social agencies may well find it desirable also to keep records of responses and registrations directly traceable to specific communication efforts. This can be helpful in deciding for the future whether to put money into direct mailing, radio announcements, or staff time in making telephone and personal calls. Often it can be a combination of exposures—a folder mailed with letter plus telephone call which produces results.

Basically, an agency communication professional has two methods of controlling costs: dollar budgeting and innovative communication methods. Used with cost/benefit estimates and analysis of communication results, these can keep communication costs to a minimum for specific communication goals.

Budgeting for Cost Control

Some organizations appropriate a lump sum yearly for all communication expenses. Without an unchanging program and unchanging goals from year to year, this is extremely difficult to do with precision and expend effectively. Even with a stable organization and program—a rare phenomenon in today's changeable society—situations alter the communication climate, calling for additional effort.

An alternate method is to appropriate money for every communication program as it arises and the need can be measured. This is based on cost/benefit estimates so that each promotion effort, for example, must be justified upon the basis of estimates of expected registrations or memberships which it can produce. Experience from year to year will make this possible with greater accuracy.

One non-profit organization uses a combination of these methods: A general appropriation to cover staff and overhead for the communication function, together with a modest sum for use as emergency supplement or for institutional image promotion. All other communication budgets are planned individually for the activity or program and are related to the specific target.

Under this method, whenever a new program such as swimming instruction mentioned in an earlier chapter is to be undertaken, the communication director will plan an appropriate promotion budget to be carried out under his/her direction. Although the budget will be approved as part of the program package, this portion will not be under the program director's control.

Standard methods of planning and promotion as described previously place emphasis on stating targets in terms of numbers of inquiries, registrations, moneys to be received; determining location of potential members or registrants, media to reach them, methods and costs; monitoring results; analyzing and changing communication tactics when necessary.

Where the effort will be sizeable and time permits, it is desirable to test a promotion on a fraction of the total and examine the results to see whether some overlooked defect can be corrected to make it more effective.

Whether or not this is possible, copy can be tested on a handful of representative prospects by reading it to them or having them read it and comment. Other cost saving efforts include:

- Consider whether you have included an effective "hook," a reason for prospects to act promptly. (See chapter on promotion.)

- Check timing—too early mailings, for example, sometimes lack response because people are not yet ready to make decisions, and expense of followup must be incurred.

- Support mailings with publicity. News media respond to appeals for space on public service programs, but publicity alone will not carry the burden.

- Consider rifled, rather than broadcast, mailings. High postage costs suggest more careful selection of prospects and prospect lists.

- Review whether catalog or multiple mailing approach may be appropriate. Where an organization has a variety of programs appealing to all ages and sexes of family, a mailing to families promoting several or more programs may obtain family-wide responses.

Consider putting volunteers on phones to inquire why—when response is slow—or to determine whether one group or another may be good prospects.

Economy Through Innovative Communication

Sometimes little or no money is available for a much needed communication effort. Such times call for resourcefulness and use of the specialist's imagination. Also, offbeat and innovative methods of communication are often more effective than the traditional ones.

Assume you have identified your target audience and have your message clearly in mind, but no budget. Ask yourself: Where may these people be found together? Can an announcement be read—at work, in school, in church? If they are not to be reached in one or several places, what other type of common exposure or way of getting information do they have? Commuter hour publicity for reaching automobile drivers? Word of mouth? Telephone relay by volunteers—each one called, calling two others? Here are a few other ideas:

- Have a prominent person in your organization write a letter to the editor of the newspaper. You write the letter and have him/her change the wording to suit his/her style before signing. Type on his/her personal stationery. Advocates and adversaries of controversial legislation have used this method effectively.

- Organize a person-to-person letter writing campaign among your constituents.

- Offer a good speaker on the subject for programs of service clubs, women's groups and others. This can generate valuable publicity as a plus factor.

- Train women and/or men volunteers to tell the story in a telephone campaign. They can identify prospects for you.

- Stage a demonstration to which the public is invited and for which news media will be interested to publish announcements and follow-up articles.

The list is endless when the imagination is set to work. The point is to decide which of the many possibilities is most appropriate, most attention compelling, most effective communication for your situation.

Cost Saving Case Histories

- **Rifling mailings.** An agency which issued a catalog of services to all members found its postage bills rising and its communication effectiveness less than desirable. It canvassed members for fields of interest, then mailed small folders on each program only to those interested, saving printing costs as well as postage. It found this increased effectiveness.

- **Compress the message.** An institution which had been putting out an expensive periodical for member communication, spent much time making it more effective—with illustrations, boxes and other layout devices. Indexing was introduced. But shortage of help caused delays in publication, missed deadlines, notices received too late for response by membership. Postal rate rises caused management to consider and finally adopt a brief mimeographed newsletter issued more frequently. The change caused favorable comments and more effective communication.

- **Postal cards.** Used for meeting date reminders, they attracted more attention, took less postage than letters.

- **Service column.** One YMCA offered a weekly "Y Corner" to its local free distribution newspaper. The editor was happy to get it. It described each week one program of the "Y" in which readers might participate, written by the program's director: aquatics, pre-school, physical fitness, Old Guard, youth leadership and the like.

- **Piggyback.** An organization with little budget for member relations persuaded an airline to add one question to a list it mailed to the organization's members in promoting travel to its annual convention. The organization consisted of professional women and its officers wanted to know whether the household help problem was serious for many constituents. A tremendous response convinced the leadership that this subject should be a major program area in future planning.

- **Enlist natural allies.** When trying to find a potential prospect list, consider which other groups share some common interest, and how by assisting you, they can benefit themselves in turn. One association attempting to launch swimming instruction programs won the help of companies selling swimming pools. They were interested in promoting water safety and widening interest in swimming generally in order to increase the potential for future sales of pools.

CHAPTER XVIII

COMMUNICATION IN ACTION—
FROM IDEAS TO COMPLETION

Middleville YMCA Board of Directors was assembling for its monthly meeting. As the members waited for latecomers the conversation was about a child's accidental drowning headlined in the evening newspaper.

"It's disgraceful!" said George White. "Every child in this community should be taught swimming and water safety from an early age."

"Maybe the schools should have a compulsory course," Charley Novak suggested.

"They'd need a pool for the winter season," Bert Lusk objected. "That means a bond issue and construction. That would take some time. I don't think people would go for it when money is tight like now."

Chairman Russ Day ended the discussion by calling for order and insisted on following the agenda. So it wasn't until new business was permitted that someone turned to Stan Holt to inquire whether the "Y" couldn't use more business for its pool. As executive director, Stan thought of the revenue situation and observed that it certainly could.

Then there was the question of scheduling—conflicts with school hours and with other groups which had already blocked off pool time for the coming season. But this picture emerged. The Y already had a community reputation for its swimming and water safety programs at summer camp. Last year's program had received an award. It had a pool already and could train a number of youngsters before next spring's outdoor season. By a consensus they directed Stan to look into the matter and report back at the next meeting.

One month later the excitement had died down. But George White had not forgotten. He wanted to hear Stan's report before taking up routine matters, but was called to order by Chairman Day. Russ knew the pool discussion might be lengthy and he wanted to make certain other matters were disposed of before they were forgotten. He welcomed Ruth Birch as first woman member of the board and suggested that it would be good to have a female viewpoint on the proposed enlargement of its swimming courses.

Under old business, Russ called for a report from the executive secretary. Stan was encouraging. He had brought Carl Kraemer, his physical education director, to the meeting to answer questions of details and to get the board's thinking about the proposed program.

* * * *

Stan reported what they had done and what they had learned. First they had decided to find out whether the community would really be interested. Had the drowning accident made enough people conscious of the need to ensure its support financially? Would enthusiasm hold up for a year-round project? Should it be extended to girls as well as boys? To older members of the family? How would they find the prospects?

There had also been the questions of scheduling. Would the schools permit youngsters to attend during school hours? The objective would be to keep the pool in use as many hours of the day as possible. What would they do about classes for the handicapped, open swimming for members and leased hours by other organizations which had been in effect for several years?

They had listed their questions, but the list seemed endless. Before spending too much time on the project, could they find the qualified instructors needed for an extended schedule? Were enough available at the hours for the classes? Wouldn't they need a full-time aquatics director to coordinate the program and what charges would be necessary to support the increased overhead including office paper work?

Stan and Carl had roughed out a budget for an estimated number of enrollees, allowing a margin for the unforeseen, and set a course fee for 10 weeks of instruction. At this point they had telephoned for Joe Rush, the public relations director to join them.

As they had outlined their plans, Joe grew enthusiastic. Together they went over the things they would need to know and wrote down questions for a survey which would help them find the answers. As they reviewed what they had written, they realized that there were more questions than people might be expected to answer readily and eliminated the less important ones.

How to communicate with potential swimming students? People had been buying backyard pools in growing numbers so there must be a lot of interest in swimming, Carl observed. "The very people to contact!" Stan remarked. If they would spend substantial amounts for pools for their children, they should be willing to spend a few more dollars to teach them how to use them safely.

All pool owners had to have municipal licenses, Joe observed. Their names and addresses would be on record at the municipal building, but it might take quite a while to go through the records and copy them. "Even better, why not ask the pool dealers for their customer lists?" asked Stan.

A man of action, he picked up the telephone book, turned to the Classified Section and dialed the first number listed under "Swimming Pools." When the manager came to the telephone, he explained what the Y was considering. Would the dealer be willing to lend his list for the purpose of sending an announcement of the proposed swimming courses?

The manager enthused as he listened. He certainly would. He could see that the courses would not only help present customers to enjoy their pools with a feeling of safety but could also create a desire for more swimming pools among those who had not purchased one.

Stan put the telephone back on its cradle. "There's your survey list," he told Joe. "You contact the other pool dealers. When you get all the lists, we'll give a last look at the questionnaire before mailing it."

Within a few days Joe had all the lists, although he had to visit some dealers personally to pick up ones which had not been forwarded. As soon as dealers realized he was not a competitor, Joe found they were glad to cooperate. Some suggested that they would like to have copies of the list of those who signed up to mail announcements of their own. Realizing he would be publishing such a list anyway and thinking of the possibility of a donated prize for Achievement Day at season's end, he agreed.

In checking with the executive director before mailing out the questionnaire, Joe mentioned the request from the pool dealer and his thought about getting prizes donated for an achievement ceremony in the spring. Such an event would have interest for the newspapers he expected. Stan nodded. He showed Joe that he had already filled out in pencil a Management-by-Objective (MBO) Chart with tentative dates.

"Of course," he said, "this all depends on the results of your survey and the approval of the board. But at this point I'd say prospects look good."

Stan looked over the questionnaire, also the letter to accompany it which would carry a printed signature of the board chairman. The letter asked for the pool owner's cooperation in filling out and promptly returning it. Joe had added a final question: "Would you be interested in receiving announcements of the swimming course schedules and fees? Yes____ No____."

"It looks fine," said Stan, "but since Russ' name will be signed, give him a call and ask if he wants to see it before you process it."

The letter was approved and went out the following day. As he awaited the results, Joe called Carl to inform him that the survey was under way and to inquire whether he had had any luck in finding personnel. When his report was encouraging, Joe decided it was time to set up his own chart for Communication-By-Objective. Referring to Stan's MBO chart, he prepared a time table for everything affecting the public relations department.

In his own planning, Joe noted the maximum tentative estimates of the number of persons who would be accommodated in courses for the first ten-week period. He wrote down this number as his goal for the tentative opening date. With this in mind, he began calculating what promotion would be needed to achieve a capacity group of students.

He had mailed out 300 questionnaires. In national mailings, he knew a three per cent return is often considered good. But his mailing was to an already interested group. It was possible he might receive 10, even 50 per cent replies. Of course summer vacation absences might delay answers. But he would expect pool owners to remain home in the summer. He noted on his calendar to initiate a telephone follow up if questionnaires were not returned in numbers by the following week. Remembering the mailing had included a business reply envelope which should boost his returns, he set a goal of 40 answers by the next board meeting.

Joe reviewed his publicity needs: Announcements to newspapers, radio and television of the courses with requirements for admission, dates and schedule; announcement of new aquatics director with photo if approved and appointed; mail invitation to prospects; opening day announcement with arrangements for press photographers to get pictures; announcements to be read in the schools and in churches. Beside each he jotted down a rough estimate of budget for postage, preparation and processing.

A phone call from Stan interrupted his planning. He would like a meeting with Carl and him the following Monday morning to review where they stood on the swimming project. As Joe noted it on his calendar, he observed that it might be early to tell anything from mailing returns.

Monday's mail, however, brought a number of replies which Joe grabbed as he left for the meeting. As might be expected the first respondents were enthusiastic and all wanted further information. Swimmers and would-be swimmers averaged two children and two adults per family but one had five boys and girls. Would they have family rates, Joe wondered.

Stan first called on Carl to advise of his success in finding instructors. It appeared that there were a number of qualified persons in the community who might be willing to teach a few courses each week, including homemakers who might prefer to teach while their own children were in school.

Carl had talked with the present part-time aquatics program director, but had found him unreceptive to working full time. He had a job as car salesman and, now that business was picking up, would like to give up the Y job in the near future. This left them free to hire someone else full time if they could find such a person. Carl had several possibilities, but was afraid the salary needed was too high. One, with several years' experience, was already employed, but was unhappy where he was.

On the matter of salary, Stan observed that he perhaps had a resource he had not revealed if the survey showed a strong need for the courses. He had talked with the superintendent of schools—later with the high school principal and his physical education director. They were friendly toward the project. They felt that daytime classes for students could be worked out by excusing those who elected swimming instruction to attend classes at the Y. They might even move the students with school buses for the assigned periods which would enable them to keep them under their supervision. The physical education director promised to take the matter up with the elementary school principal who had not been able to make their luncheon discussion.

As Stan had talked with the superintendent of schools in the beginning, they had considered the matter of school credit for the classes. For this purpose, the superintendent had noted, they would need someone to direct the program whose qualifications were recognized by the State Education Department. The more they considered it, the more feasible it seemed to employ a highly qualified aquatics director whose salary might be higher than Stan had budgeted. Could the board of education under these circumstances help out some way? The superintendent suggested that, although they had no budget, perhaps they could find enough to pay half the salary and give the man or woman an academic appointment.

When Joe showed his publicity plans, Stan had a further suggestion. "Let's build enthusiasm by having a Recognition Day half way through the courses when the students show how far they have advanced before their friends and other invited guests," he said. "That way we'll help them renew their own enthusiasm about the time it is beginning to wear a little, and we'll develop our prospects for the next swim period. Achievement Day when we pass out the certificates will come at year's end."

* * * * *

As the executive director reviewed the highlights of this progress at the second board meeting, he was also able to tell them that the results of the test survey were very encouraging. Just to make certain they would have something solid to report, Joe and his assistants had made a score of phone calls to prospects who had failed to reply.

With questionnaire before them they had asked and jotted down answers for each family. From their findings Carl planned to add swim preparation periods for pre-school children with their mothers to give them confidence in the water. They had also included swimming for physical fitness courses for senior citizens, homemakers and executives.

As Stan summarized his conversations with the school people

the board listened intently. It appeared that there had been some demand for swimming in the schools. The board of education members seemed favorable to paying part of the director's salary if he was also qualified to coach a swimming team. At this point George White began to object. If their aquatics director were to be a coach, there was the danger that he would be more interested in producing potential athletes than providing swimming proficiency to all youngsters, he said.

The chairman turned to his new board member. How did the proposed program impress her? Ruth had talked with Stan about it on the telephone and had made arrangements to examine the visiting team dressing facilities before the meeting. If they were to have girls as well as boys in the program, she felt, they would need to add several toilets and showers. This would be particularly true for all-girl classes. While they might get along with coed classes for now, this was something to be considered for the future.

This introduced a new element which board members discussed at length. Finally, they decided that the imperative thing was to get a program under way. If the program grew, they might consider the new implications of building alterations. They authorized the chairman and executive director to employ an aquatics director—jointly with the schools if possible but with the understanding that any matter of team coaching would have to wait until the program was solidly launched. They directed Russ to call a special meeting or consult members by telephone, if any major hitch or new direction seemed to call for it, before the next regular meeting and to aim for a beginning soon after school reopening in September.

With this approval, Stan and Joe adjusted and finalized their charts. Joe prepared to set his promotional efforts in motion as soon as survey results were tabulated and analyzed. He also made a note to arrange for the new aquatics director to speak on the radio, in the schools and before service club groups as soon as he was able to become grounded in his new assignment. He made a note on his March calender to send a letter to all swimming pool dealers to thank them in the name of the chairman for their cooperation, to report on the results and to announce plans for Achievement Day. At the same time he would invite them to offer prizes for competitions and to attend the ceremonies.

CHAPTER XIX

PR CREATES LOW-BUDGET REVOLUTION

In 1960 the United States Government issued a postage stamp with the slogan, "Employ the Handicapped." Business secretaries affixing the stamps to outgoing letters were unconsciously acknowledging the achievements of one of the most successful public relations programs in the nation's history.

Fifteen years, beginning in 1945, had seen a small group of dedicated men and women in the nation's capital stage a quiet revolution. With the backing of successive U.S. Presidents, they had set about reversing nationwide prejudice against a segment of the population.

So well had they succeeded that the Hire-the-Handicapped movement became recognized as almost as popular and sacredly American as motherhood and apple pie. The amazing aspect of this was that this group, the President's Committee on Employment of the Physically Handicapped, had no laws to enforce its will, little budget, and no power base except the backing of the U.S. Chief Executive and the moral persuasion of fairness.

Following World War II, the disabled coming out of military hospitals were re-trained by the Veterans Administration. Finding jobs was another matter. To consider this problem, representatives of business and the professions were assembled in Washington in 1946. They formed what was to become established by President Harry S. Truman as The President's Committee, modestly funded by the Congress.

The previous year, the first "National Employ the Physically Handicapped Week" had been held by Congressional decree. Its purpose was to dramatize the problem. The volunteer group in its first meeting decided to build on that initial educational effort. It discarded any idea of legal quotas for the handicapped. This device had been tried in Europe and had failed. It proved demeaning to the persons so employed and frustrating to the employers.

Instead, seeking a voluntary approach, the Committee adopted what was to become an extensive public relations program. It would set up no new large bureaucracy, nor ask for large appropriations of tax moneys. Instead, it would enlist the cooperation of labor and management, state and local agencies, civic and religious associations, veterans organizations and others who themselves were to provide most of the tools that were needed. Within government, the small staff scrounged office space from the Labor Department and staff services from the Veterans Administration.

While its immediate goal was to increase jobs available to handicapped persons, The Committee recognized the problems as deep-seated and wide-ranging. It saw that prejudices against handicapped persons were based on instinctive revulsion toward visible handicaps and stemmed from their own fears of becoming crippled themselves.

Skeptical employers would require completely physically fit persons whether or not this was pertinent to the specific job. Employees would resist working beside an amputee; they felt that this denigrated their own work somehow or that they might have to perform the other's work in addition to their own. Foremen particularly resented assignment of handicapped persons to their units, feeling that they would have to be "nursemaid" to those who were crippled. They also felt that if they were to be held accountable for production goals, they were entitled to workers who could turn out the best.

There were rumors about handicapped persons having poor attendance records at work, being susceptible to safety hazards and requiring special facilities. The Committee decided to get the facts and expose the myths. Fortunately, statistics enabled them to do this easily. Handicapped persons were found in many instances to have superior records of safety, attendance and productivity. In some work areas, handicaps were found to be assets—deafness in high noise areas and blindness in darkrooms and situations requiring sensitive touch.

The Committee's major decision was to emphasize the positive—what the handicapped could do for an employer. This philosophy which became widely accepted by management was:
"The handicapped person, when properly placed on a job for which he is fitted, is no longer handicapped."

The President's Committee's approach caused management people to think through more carefully the requirements of each job. One manufacturer who went "all out" to find jobs for handicapped persons cited these cases:

A wheel-chair accident victim, after 18 months' training in six departments, was assigned to handling telephone inquiries. As expected, he took a load off the shoulders of the overworked Sales Engineering Department.

A girl with crippled hands, after training in the local library, became an excellent company librarian. Her work served as a resource in support of the electrical engineering staff and sales engineers.

The company's president commented that, while he did not think the company had done a great deal, it seemed to have created many dividends of goodwill toward the company for the trouble expended in employing the handicapped.

Other companies were to find extra dividends from the new way of looking at job requirements, resulting in better placement of all personnel. This achieved better morale, increased efficiency and reduced interpersonal friction.

In the Committee's early days there was reluctance about publicizing handicapped placements on the part of some employers. They were fearful that if it was known that they employed some handicapped, they would be swamped with applicants.

Then Philadelphia celebrated National Employ the Physically Handicapped Week with a parade. Floats sponsored by individual companies showed handicapped employees demonstrating their operation of machines. Another myth was exploded! The handicapped people were given pride in their achievements in place of hiding their disability from embarrassment.

Commented one employer: "Too many handicapped? The more the better!"

At its annual meeting, The President's Committee began to honor the "Handicapped American of the Year." Without seeking credit for itself, the Committee continually recognized others for the excellent work they were doing in support of The Committee's objectives: people in industry and labor, corporations, associations. Television and radio gave millions of dollars' worth of air time—newspapers, of space. A blimp with flashing lights proclaimed, "Hire the Handicapped—It's Good

Business!" Companies sponsored motion pictures showing handicapped persons' work achievements as inspiration for others. Perhaps the ultimate was a film news story of a quadraplegic who started and successfully operated a business of his own.

In every way thinkable, the Committee's staff sought to keep the problem and the solutions dramatically in people's minds. It never seemed to lack volunteers from the professions or the media to assist when special talent or know-how was required. The trade press proved a valuable asset.

As the Committee's chairman, a retired, blind Marine Corps officer, remarked:

"The fine contribution of the handicapped themselves has been a key to the success of the undertaking. The handicapped have justified the confidence placed in them. They have more than measured up to expectations."

In later years, the Committee changed its name by dropping the word "physically" and has taken on the task of a similar public relations job for the mentally restored and the mentally retarded. Here the problem, although different, has met with similar success.

Once, around 1960, the Committee's achievement was called the most memorable development of the century with its destruction of a stereotype and its reversal of a public attitude toward a disadvantaged minority without substantial opposition.

From the Committee's experience, these lessons in communication and public relations can be noted:

• With a small professional staff and high volunteer input it is possible to achieve a major social objective without a large budget or legal imperatives.

• Cooperation from others is forthcoming when they recognize a common advantage and an absence of competition for budget moneys and power.

• To enlist support, work through established agencies and give them the credit wherever possible.

• Obtain a high priority rating from the establishment—in a community campaign involve the mayor and other leading citizens.

- Identify the roadblocks to action; get the facts; clear away the myths; confront the situation as it exists.

- Focus on the positive—what the goal's achievement can mean to the beneficiaries, thus diverting attention from imaginary fears and reservations.

- Involve not only natural allies but also leaders of groups where difficulties lie (as the Committee did with employers and employees), and persuade them to educate their own groups.

- Dramatize and make visible every advance toward the goal with forms of recognition and by all communication media and methods available.

- Be generous with honors and commendations of others who cooperate and assist. The Committee created a number of awards such as "Handicapped Employer of the Year."

As Emerson said, "There's no limit to what can be accomplished if it doesn't matter who gets the credit."

Since The President's Committee was started in 1945, we have seen several social revolutions occur. We might today disagree with the observer who in 1960 characterized progress in turning physically handicapped persons into self-supporting citizens as "the greatest advancement in the social field since World War II." But few other major revolutions in society have occurred with so little opposition and at so little cost to society.

This desirable revolution was accomplished by "pure public relations."

APPENDIX

MEDIA SELECTION GUIDELINES

Choosing the media or methods by which to convey a message requires consideration of such factors as:

Availability—Do you have ready access without great difficulty to a printer, a newspaper, a radio or television station? Do you have a membership publication already in being? Can you set up a telephone relay organization without incurring toll calls through other exchanges?

Audience potential—Does the medium reach large numbers of persons you wish to reach? Are they accustomed to getting information through this medium so that they will listen to, or read your message?

Message control—Do you have complete decision as to the form in which your message will go out as in a printed brochure or advertisement? Or do you have to filter your message through other persons who may misquote or mistranslate your message through misunderstanding as sometimes in newspaper reporting? Can you minimize this hazard through press releases? Is the hazard minimal?

Impact—Is the medium one which influences readers or listeners in their thinking and actions because of its prestige and reputation? Does it lend itself to making the kind of impression you want to make? (Would you pick the society page to advertise a baseball game benefit?)

The executive or communication professional will consider these factors in relation to:

The nature of the message—Is it brief or does it require extensive explanation? It might call for a bumper sticker or a symposium—or something in between. Does it require showing as well as telling?

The Target—Is it one person, a few people, or as many responders as possible?

The feedback requirements—inquiries, applications, donations, voluntary enlistments, public support in letters, phone calls or other direct action? Some publications would not print a post office address to which to write or a telephone number to call in editorial space; this suggests advertising. If immediate response is wanted, one would avoid less frequent publications for those which people read less leisurely. Or one might turn to electronic media with its feeling of immediacy.

The nature of the goal—Peer influence? Action? Long-range or short-range? An appeal for a capital gift is long-range compared to a solicitation for an annual gift and suggests a medium providing extensive material to be digested over a long period of time as one essential.

Preparation requirements—Is message preparation simple or extensive and time-consuming? Do the potential results justify media requirements in terms of total cost? A mimeographed press release may require a day for writing, checking and processing—a film clip for television several days of writing, casting, rehearsing, photographing. But the latter may be used several times—and if not dated, over an extensive period.

The 4H association, whose festival is mentioned elsewhere, engages in year-round planning and preparation. But its proved audience potential reaches well into thousands of prime potential prospects for membership. Its impact is of the highest—visual plus audio; it eliminates all media filtering of its message by placing its audience directly in contact with its programs in action. Its message becomes an experience, something more than show-and-tell.

For those with less varied communication experience, the following check list of media characteristics may be helpful. It lists some more commonly used media along with a few less used media in the agency field to stimulate the imagination and invention of communication professionals.

Medium or Method	Advantages	Disadvantages
Person to person	Prompt feedback Personal rather than impersonal Complete attention—generally Potential for negotiation	No record No reruns One receiver only Time consuming

Medium or Method	Advantages	Disadvantages
Telephoning	Prompt feedback Personal rather than impersonal Potential for negotiation Cost, if local	Recording is time consuming, perhaps embarrassing No reruns One or few receivers Cost, if long distance
Letter (Personal)	Personal On the record Chance for rereading, changing	Single recipient Time consuming Delayed response Cost
Letter (Form)	Record Rereading Many recipients Time savings Cost	Impersonal Shotgun approach Delayed response Time for processing Cost
Brochure	Eye appeal Extensive presentation Many recipients Permanent record	Cost Preparation time Delayed response Impersonal Shotgun approach
Meeting	No media filter Peer influence Prompt feedback Full feedback Negotiation potential	Difficulty of arranging Cost Variable impact Preparation time Time consuming
Radio	Low production costs for. . . Mass audience Immediacy Appeal to imagination Little preparation	Lack of visual image Modestly difficult feedback No record with receiver for future reference
Television	Mass audience Video and audio	Modestly difficult feedback

Medium or Method	Advantages	Disadvantages
Television (continued)	High impact Built-in appeal	No record with receiver High cost Major preparation
Newspaper	Mass audience On the record Timeliness Prompt feedback	No audio
--Advertising	Copy control Timing control Easy feedback Assured use	Cost Advance ordering Less attention compelling than news item
--Publicity release	Low cost Little preparation 3rd party evaluation	No assurance of use Lack of feedback information Lack of message control No copy control
Magazines and Journals	Selective audiences Extensive treatment Longer impact	Less frequent publication Early preparation Delayed responses
--Advertising vs. Publicity	Similar to newspapers	Newspapers similar (see above)
Recordings	Novelty appeal Mass audience Low cost Audio On the record Controlled audience Personalized, if wished	Not everyone has a record player Short life No visual Requires receiver's effort

Medium or Method	Advantages	Disadvantages
Bumper stickers	Punchy message Little preparation Mass use lowers cost Long life	No explanation -- slogan only No assured feedback
Posters	High visibility Selected locations	Time for placement Essentially static
--Hand made	Flexibility of design Eye catching	Extensive preparation No record for viewer
--Printed	Mass coverage	Higher lead time
Sidewalk easels (enlarged two-directional posters)	Catch pedestrian attention	Not permitted everywhere
Sandwich signs	More attention compelling than static easels	Time and cost No record for receiver
Handbills and flyers	Record for later reference of receiver Timing control	Cost of preparation Cost of distribution Impermanence
Telephone Relay	Quick communication Member involvement Prompt feedback	Organizing time Message dilution hazard Uncertainties of volunteer performance
Festival	Show and tell Complete presentation Audience participation Member participation	Long range preparation Volunteer performance

Medium or Method	Advantages	Disadvantages
Membership Publication	Regularity of communication	Staff time and preparation
	Establishes reader habits	Distribution costs
	Control of contents	

Imaginative media use attracts attention and assures that a message will get through. Few agencies would normally consider having volunteers act as sandwich bearers and pass out handbills as a way of getting a crowd to attend a benefit concert or sports event. Yet on a big shopping day with crowds in town —or a Saturday in a shopping mall—this might be the one communication which would grab attention and secure a sizeable turnout.

The point is to canvass all communication resources and then use them in unexpected ways which make your point.

COMMUNICATION RESOURCE BOOKS

Because of limited space in this text, many aspects of communication and related subjects could not be pursued in depth. For readers who wish to pursue these fields of communication further, the following books may be found helpful.

MBO FOR NON-PROFIT ORGANIZATIONS. Dale D. McConkey. New York: Amacon, a Division of American Management Association, 135 West 50th Street, New York, N.Y. 10020. 240pp. A business executive, based on his experience as volunteer leader of community service organizations, tells how management by objective techniques used in business are adapted for service-oriented agencies. 1975.

COMPLETE GUIDE TO PASTEUP. Walter B. Graham. Philadelphia: North American Publishing Co. 247pp. Elaborately illustrated text shows how to prepare copy for camera, ideas for layout and related matters. 1975.

COMMUNICATION METHODS FOR ALL MEDIA. Hadley Read. Urbana, Ill.: University of Illinois Press. 308pp. Excellent text and reference work for professionals and would-be-professionals. 1972.

GUIDE TO SUCCESSFUL FUND-RAISING. Bernard P. Taylor. South Plainfield, N.J.: Groupwork Today, Inc. 134pp. The author has here summarized basic approaches and techniques which he used successfully in 27 colleges and universities and taught in his Fund Raising Workshop at Chautauqua Institution to college presidents and fund-raising professionals representing a variety of institutions. 1976.

THE SPEECH WRITING GUIDE. James J. Welch. New York: John J. Wiley & Sons. 128pp. Compact, lively, comprehensive in scope, this book gives "do's and don'ts" with hints for effectiveness, time estimating, rehearsal, delivery, use of audio-visuals, supplemental benefits. Reference section is excellent with helpful check lists. 1968.

HOW TO SPEAK THE WRITTEN WORD. Nedra Newkirk Lamar. Old Tappan, N.J.: Fleming H. Revell Co. 192pp. The author, an instructor and coach of public readers, emphasizes thoughts expressed in the written word and how to convey them to an audience. Final section is devoted to Bible reading. Revised 1967.

THE MODERN BUSINESS LETTER WRITER'S MANUAL. Marjane Cloker and Robert Wallace. Garden City, N.Y.: Doubleday. 215pp. Refreshing approach to making letters communicate, dispensing with formalities and obfuscation. 1969.

HOW TO READ A PERSON LIKE A BOOK. Gerard I. Nierenberg. New York: Hawthorne Books. 185pp. How observations of facial expressions and body language can reveal a person's inner feelings, making listening more intelligent and personal communication possible. 1971.

THE ART OF NEGOTIATING. Gerard I. Nierenberg. New York: Hawthorne Books. 195pp. Methods and strategies for arriving at agreements through effective communication. 1968.

YOUR OWN GROUPWORK AGENCY STUDY. Harry E. Moore, Jr. 92pp. North Plainfield, N.J.: Galloway Corp. Helpful guidelines for evaluating an agency's communication activities as well as its total effectiveness. Helps determine communication needs and objectives. 1974.

INDEX

American Red Cross, 5, 27,126
Annual reports, 110, 147-152
Applications, acknowledging, 136
Board chairperson, 15-16, 102-103, 115
Board, governing, 14-16, 100-105
  meetings, 100-102
  orientation, 101-102
  reports to, 104-105
Boy Scouts of America, 6,8,9,111
Brainstorming, 67,72
Budgeting, 154-155
Camp promotion, 38-41, 138-140
Case histories, 7,12,15, 17,19-21,25,26,107, 112-113,119-120,120-122, 132,135,156-157,165-169
Case of Incomplete Listening, 107-108
Case of Lost Identity, 25-26
Channels, 120-121
Checklists, 109,113,118, 136,146
Chief executive as communicator, 11-17, 102-103
Churches, 123-126,132,133
Climate for communication, 23
Communication
  in a changing organization, 11, 29-31
  nature of organizational, 12
  need for continuous flow, 32
  role of chief executive, 12,102-103
  with governing board, 14, 104-105

Communication (cont'd)
  with leadership, 50-51
  with professionals, 48-49
  with volunteers, 49-51
Communication by objectives
  defined, 2
  external, 3-4
  four steps in, 2-3
  importance of, 4
  in action, 18-21,158-164
  in external communication, 22-32
  internal, 2-3
  organization for, 36-38
  planning for, 36-38
  purpose of, 2
Communication channels, 12-13, 120-121
Community involvement, 18
Compliments, handling, 117-118
Conversation stoppers, 52-54
Cost control, 153-157
Cost savings, 156-157
Crisis communication
  need for honesty, 25
  solid image as asset, 10, 25
Criticism, 51-52, 106
  dealing with, 106
  turning critics into supporters, 51-52
Dialogue, 114,116
Drawings, 93-94
Economy, 153-157
Efficiency in staff meeting 69
Employee relations, 114, 117
Examples, 111, 116, 118, 120-122, 123-126, 129-131, 158-164
Executive, characteristics of successful, 1

177

Executive as communicator
  importance of communication skill, 1-4, 12-13
  responsibilities of, 12-13
Executive health club, 129-131
External communication, 3-4
Feedback, 23, 40-41, 48, 70-71, 131-133, 144
  in personal communication, 48
  through staff meetings, 70-71
Follow up, 135-136
4-H Club, 133-134
Fund raising, 100, 108-113
Girard College, 25-26
Girl Scouts, 121-122
Giving, reasons for, 109
Goals, 9-10, 19-20, 37, 140
  defining, 37
  in image building, 9-10
  setting targets, 19-20
Governing Board (see Board, Governing)
Green Circle program, 122
Group meetings, 140
Groups, communication with, 114-118
Guidelines, 6-7
  as substitute for image, 7
  importance to communicators, 6
  in new organizations, 7
High priority communication, 99-113
Hobby fair, 133-134
Image building, 5, 8-10, 24, 27-29, 109-110, 114-115, 119-120, 122
  as communication objective, 5
  endless task, 24
  goals in, 9-10
  importance of consistency, 114-115
  name as symbol, 9
  publicity in, 10

Image building (cont'd)
  rating an image, 9
  revision of image, 8-9, 24-32
  steps for, 28-29
  telephone communication in, 10
  through negotiation, 117
  value of dramatic objective in, 10
  value of symbols, 27
  value in fund raising, 109-110
"In-groups," 99
Information circle, 11-16
Innovative communication, 155-156
Insider groups, 14, 99
Internal communication, four steps in, 2-3
Jewish Community Center, 15
Job assignments, 71
Leadership training, 120-122
Learning for Living, 132
Listening, 125
Management by objective, 2
Maslow, Abraham, 47
Meals on Wheels, 132
Meetings,
  Board, 100-102
  Staff, 67-73
Membership building, 127-137
Membership communication, 137
Monitoring results, 4, 70-71
Morale, 70
Mutual benefits, 31, 126
Mystery of the Missing Members, 135
Myths, dispelling, 150-151
National Foundation for Infantile Paralysis, 27
Negotiating, 115, 122-126
New Ideas, presenting, 46, 106
New members, 136
Newsletter, 141
Objectives, 13-14, 22, 122-126
  external communication, 22

Objectives (cont'd)
  internal communication, 13-14
  sharing, 122-126
Obstacles to communication, 23, 27, 28, 45-46, 52-53
  conversation stoppers, 52-53
  fuzzy image, 27, 28
  prejudice, 45-46
Orientation of the new trustee, 15
Overhead expenses, justifying, 111
PR Creates Low Budget Revolution, 165-169
Person-to-person communication, 42-48, 100, 102-103, 105-106, 115, 134-136
  base point for media evaluation, 42
  characteristics of, 42-43
  controlling conversational direction, 45
  establishing climate for, 47
  for avoiding misunderstandings, 48
  for clarifying question, 43, 134-136
  for handling prejudice, 45-46
  for presenting new ideas, 46
  planning for, 43
  probing for causes, 43
  sensitivity, importance of, 43-44
  stating agreement, 48
Personal style in media choice, 17
Personnel for communication, 33-41
  choosing spokesperson, 33
  dividing responsibilities, 33
  in action, 38-41
  preparation for assignment, 36-38
  requirements and personal assets of, 34

Personnel (cont'd)
  selecting a director, 33-35
Persuasive communication, 89-91
Photography, 92-98
  captions, 95-96
  honesty in, 95
  layouts, 97
Pictorial communication, 92-98
Platform for communication, 6, 36-37
  nature of, 6
  purpose as guidelines, 6
  writing a, 36-37
Planning communication, 16-21, 36-38, 92-97
  essentiality of, 16
  for community involvement, 18
  for interviews, 17
  in action, 19-21, 36-38, 92-97
  media selection, 17
  staff meetings, 66-73
  timing, 17
  usefulness to executive, 18
  what it does, 18
  what it requires, 19
Prejudice, 45-46, 52-53, 108, 122
  avoiding, 52-53
  overcoming, 45-46
President's Committee on Employment of the Physically Handicapped, 31, 165-169
Priorities, 99
Problem-solving, 72
Problems vs. programs, 29-30
Professionals
  communication with, 48-49
  new generation, 48-49
  problems with older staff, 49
Programs, 128-140
  as communication, 133-134

Programs (cont'd)
  promotion of, 19-21, 128-140
Promotional communication, 2,3-4, 19-21, 89-91, 128-140
  for church, 132-133
  for 4-H club, 133-134
  for health club, 129-131
  for senior citizens program, 19-21
  for summer camp, 38-41, 138-140
  of membership, 129-131
  planning for, 19-21
  telephone use in, 135-136
Prospect list, 128-129
Public relations, 23,24, 114, 117, 165-169
Publicity, 10
"Publics," defined, 116
Relationships, keys to, 114
Religious associations, 123-126
Reports, 104-105
SNAFU at the Youth Center, 12
Selling changes, 30-31
Sensitivity training, 120-122
Speakers, 74-77
  checklist for inviting, 75-77
  courtesies to be extended, 76-77
  outside, value of, 74
  preparation for, 76
  sponsor's responsibilities, 76
Speeches, 77-80
  checklist for speakers, 77-78
  delivery of, 78-79, 85
  introductions of, 86
  preparation for, 77-78
  research for, 84-85
  speaker's bureau, 79-80

Speeches (cont'd)
  typing text, 83
  use of audio-visuals, 85
  writing texts of, 81-86
  writing for own delivery, 82
  writing for someone else, 82-83
Spoken communication, 74-78, 79, 85-86
Staff meetings as communication, 66-73
  advance notice of, 68
  brainstorming, 67, 72
  concluding, 73
  efficiency in, 69
  for generating job assignments, 71
  for monitoring and feedback, 70-71
  for morale, 70
  for problem-solving, 72
  objectives of, 66
  planning sessions, 67-68
  timing, 73
  types of, 67-70
  whom to ask, 73
  with single purpose, 69
Strategy, 18, 122
Supplier relationships, 115-116
Symbols, 8-9
Synagogues, 123
Systematizing communication, 103-104
Targeting, 139-140
Telephone as medium, 55-65, 135-136
  advantages, 55, 64-65
  answering coverage, 56-57
  answering services and devices, 57
  and institutional image, 10, 57
  for feedback in promotion, 37
  guidelines for efficiency, 59-61

Telephone (cont'd)
  guidelines for success, 62-63
  handling incoming calls, 55-60
  hints for executives, 65
  importance to image, 10
  importance to management, 10
  keeping costs in line, 63-64
  planning survey, 56
  training, 57-58
  when to choose as medium, 64-65
Timing, 13-14, 120
United Way, 47, 110-111, 117, 126
Unity, 14-16, 22, 100-101
  building through communication, 14-16
  in communication goals, 14
  in communication process, 22
Viscardi, Henry, 17
Visiting Nurses Association, 8
Visual communication, 92-98
Volunteers, 49-51
Written communication, 81-91
  advantages of, 81
  avoiding misunderstandings, 88
  for silent reading, 87-91
  organization for, 82, 84-86
  persuasive writing, 89-91
  reports, 87-88
  speech introductions, 86
  speech texts, 82-86
  two types of, 81
YMCA, 6, 8, 9, 28, 134, 158-164

DATE DUE
OCT ?